Computer games

What makes a good game?

Some games have a magical quality that makes you want to play them time and again. Game designers call it playability. To make a game with great playability, you need to think about all the ingredients that make up the game and how they work together.

I have the perfect recipe!

◁ Characters

In most games, the player uses an on-screen character to enter the game world. It could be an animal, a princess, a race car, or even just a simple bubble. To create a sense of danger or competition, such games usually also have enemy characters that the player has to defeat or escape from.

△ Mechanics

These are the "verbs" in a game—actions such as running, jumping, flying, capturing objects, casting spells, and using weapons. The mechanics are the core of the game, and well-designed mechanics make a good game.

△ Objects

Nearly all games include objects, from stars and coins that boost health or scores to keys that unlock doors. Not all objects are good—some get in the player's way, sap their health, or steal their treasures. Objects can also work together to create puzzles for the player to solve.

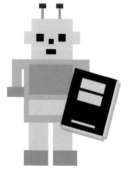

◁ Rules

The rules of a game tell you what you're allowed and not allowed to do. For example, can you walk through walls or do they block your path? Can you stop and think or do you have to beat the clock?

YOU SCORED

25,547,010

POINTS!!!

◁ **World**

Think about the world in which a game is played. Is it 2-D or 3-D? Does the player view the game from above, from the side, or from within? Does the game world have walls or boundaries that limit the player's movement or is it open like the outdoors?

△ **Goals**

Every game challenges the player to achieve some kind of goal, whether it's winning a race, conquering an enemy, beating a high score, or simply surviving for as long you can. Most games have lots of small goals, such as unlocking doors to new levels or winning new vehicles or skills.

◁ **Controls**

Keyboards, mice, joysticks, and motion sensors all make good controllers. Games are more fun when the player feels in complete control of the character, so the controls should be easy to master and the computer should respond instantly.

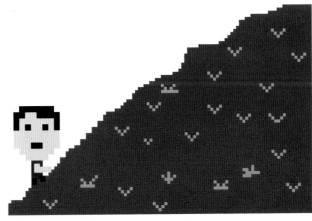

△ **Difficulty level**

A game's no fun if it's too easy or too hard. Many games make the challenges easy at the start, while the player is learning, and more difficult later as the player's skills improve. Getting the difficulty level just right is the key to making a great game.

GAME DESIGN

Playability

Games don't have to be complicated to make people want to play them over and over again. One of the first successful computer games was a simple tennis simulator called Pong. The ball was a white square and the racquets were white lines that could only move up and down. Although there were no fancy graphics, people loved Pong because it had great playability. They could compete against friends, just like in real tennis, and it was just hard enough to demand intense concentration and a steady hand, leaving players always wanting another game.

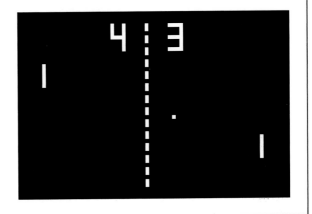

Atmosphere

A good game, just like a movie or a book, can draw you in and change the way you feel by creating a certain atmosphere. Here are some of the tricks game designers use to conjure up an atmosphere.

◁ **Telling stories**

A background story helps set the scene for a game and gives meaning to the player's actions. Blockbuster games have movielike plots with twists, but even simple games can benefit from some kind of story if it makes players feel they're on a mission. Thinking of a story also helps you give a game a consistent theme.

△ **Boo!**

Do things jump out at the player? Fear and suspense can make a game scary and put the player on edge. What's around the next corner? What's behind that door? The wait can be worse than the scare!

▷ **Sound**

Sounds can have a strong effect on how we feel. Changing the tune can make the same scene feel exciting, scary, or even silly, and a sudden noise after a quiet spell can cause a jolt of terror. Modern games use realistic sound effects to make players feel like they're inside the action.

▷ **Faster, faster!**

The speed of a game changes the level of excitement a player feels. It's easy to stay calm when you can stop and think about what to do next, but with a ticking clock and fast music, you can't help but feel under pressure.

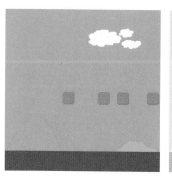

◁ **Color scheme**

You can change the atmosphere in a game simply by altering the colors. Bright blue, yellow, and green feels warm and sunny, for instance, while icy blues and white feel wintry, and darker colors make a game feel spooky.

▽ **Graphics**

The graphics in the first games were simple geometric shapes, but as computers became more powerful, the graphics in games got better. Many console games now feature photorealistic 3-D images, but games based on simple, cartoonlike graphics are as popular as ever and can help create a more playful atmosphere.

■ ■ GAME DESIGN

Virtual reality

Virtual reality goggles could make the games of the future much more realistic. They work by presenting each eye with a slightly different image, creating a 3-D experience. Motion sensors in the headset track the player's movements and adjust the images to match, allowing the player to turn around and look in any direction, just like in the real world. As a result, a player feels inside the game world instead of watching it through a screen.

Where are you?

One of the easiest ways to create atmosphere is to give a game a location by adding a background image. To make the illusion more convincing, make sure the game's characters match the setting—don't put racecars in the deep sea or unicorns in outer space, for instance.

◁ **Snow and ice**
A snowy scene is the backdrop for a race along an icy road.

△ **Spooky forest**
A dark forest is the perfect setting for ghosts, griffins, and witches.

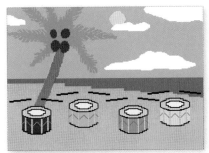

△ **Tropical beach**
A sunny beach creates a carnival mood for the colorful steel drums.

△ **Deep-sea adventure**
Octopuses and starfish fit well with this underwater scene.

Types of games

Games come in all shapes and sizes, but most fit into one of just a few main categories, called genres. Some gamers like the platform games genre best, whereas others prefer racing games or strategy games. What are your favorite genres?

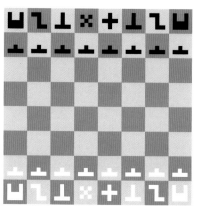

◁ **Traditional**
When you can't find an opponent to play with you, a computer can challenge you to a game of cards, chess, or a million other popular board games.

△ **Role-playing**
Dungeons, dragons, and castles feature in these adventure games. Players may roam freely or follow a set storyline, with their character developing specialized skills as it advances, such as casting spells or sword-fighting. Some role-playing games are played online, allowing lots of players to interact in the same game world.

▷ **Racing**
Racing games create the illusion of speed by making the scenery scroll past the player's viewpoint. To succeed, you need to learn each racetrack inside out so you can start tricky maneuvers in advance.

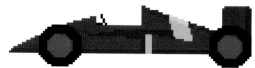

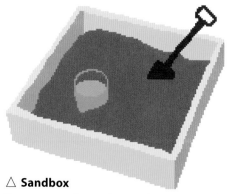

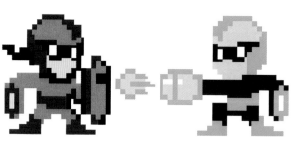

△ **Sandbox**
Some games force players along a set path, but sandbox games are the opposite: they give you complete freedom to explore the game world at your own pace and choose different quests within it.

△ **Combat**
Nimble fingerwork is vital for games involving close-quarters combat. The key to success is knowing when and how to use many different attack and defense moves, from slams and somersaults to special powers.

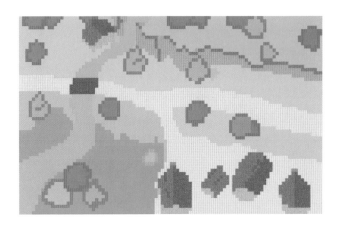

▷ **Strategy**

Decisions, decisions. What are the best choices to make if you're running a zoo, fighting a war, or building a whole civilization? Strategy games give the player godlike powers over many different characters at once, but you have to manage resources cleverly or your empire will collapse.

△ **Simulator**

If you want a puppy but don't want the trouble of feeding and walking it, a virtual pet might suit you. Simulators aim to re-create real-life situations. Some are more than just a game: flight simulators are so accurate and realistic that professional pilots use them for training.

◁ **Music and dance**

Dance-mat games involve tapping the feet or jumping over a stream of obstacles in time to the rhythm. Music games allow you to play along with a virtual band using a pretend instrument. You need to hit the right notes on time to complete each level.

△ **Sport**

Play the game of your choice as your favorite team, set in a realistic stadium with roaring crowds. Sports games let you compete in famous tournaments such as the soccer World Cup, with the computer referee ensuring fair play.

△ **Puzzle**

Some people love to exercise their brains with puzzles. There are many different types, from colorful tile-matching games to number puzzles and escape games, in which you need to use your imagination to find your way from room to room.

How coding works

A computer can't think for itself—it works by blindly following instructions. It can only carry out a complex task if that task has been broken down into simple steps that tell it exactly what to do and in what order. Writing these instructions in a language a computer understands is called coding.

Planning a game

Imagine you want to create a game in which you fly a parrot over a river, collecting apples as they drift downstream but avoiding an angry lion. You would need to give the computer a separate set of instructions for each object in the game: the apple, the parrot, and the lion.

The player makes the parrot fly left and right with the left and right arrow keys.

Pressing the space bar makes the parrot dive, but the game ends if you touch the lion.

Score   10

The player wins a point each time the parrot gets an apple.

The apple drifts downstream over and over. It reappears on the left if the parrot takes it.

The lion walks left and right, following the parrot.

▽ **Apple**
You can't simply tell the computer that the apple drifts down the river and vanishes when the parrot eats it. Instead, you need to break down this complicated task into a set of very simple steps as shown here.

Jump to the left edge of the screen.

Repeat the following steps over and over again:

  Move a bit to the right.

  If I get to the right edge of the screen then

    jump back to the left edge.

  If I touch the parrot then

    add one to the parrot's score and

    jump back to the left edge.

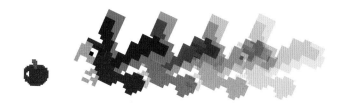

▷ **Parrot**

The parrot is more complicated than the apple because the player controls it and it can move up, down, left, and right. Even so, it's possible to make all of this work by writing a sequence of simple instructions.

Jump to the top right of the screen.

Repeat these steps in turn:

If the player presses the left arrow then

move a bit to the left if I can.

If the player presses the right arrow then

move a bit to the right if I can.

If the player presses the space bar then

move all the way to the bottom of the screen taking a second and

move all the way back to the top taking a second

▷ **Lion**

The lion is the player's enemy and can end the game if the parrot touches it. It is controlled by a simple program.

Jump to the middle of the screen.

Repeat these steps in turn:

If the parrot is to my left then

move a bit to my left.

If the parrot is to my right then

move a bit to my right.

If the parrot touches me then

stop the game.

▷▷ **LINGO**

Programming languages

The instructions on this page are in simple English, but if you wanted to create the game on a computer, you would need to translate them into special words that the computer can understand: a programming language. Writing programs with a programming language is called coding or programming. This book uses the programming language Scratch, which is ideal for learning about coding and great for making games.

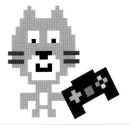

Getting started

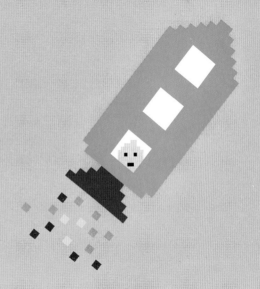

Introducing Scratch

All the games in this book are made with a programming language called Scratch. Scratch is easy to learn because you don't have to type any complicated code. Instead, you build programs from ready-made blocks.

> The characters and other objects in Scratch games are called sprites.

Starting from scratch

A project in Scratch usually starts with choosing the objects, or sprites, that will appear in the game. Scratch has a large library of sprites, or you can create your own.

Sprites

Sprites are the things that move around or react in the game. They can be anything from animals and people to pizzas or spaceships. You can bring each sprite to life on screen with a list of instructions called code.

The cat sprite appears whenever you start a new Scratch project.

Code blocks

Code is made of text blocks that you can drag with a computer mouse and join like pieces of a jigsaw puzzle. Each block has one instruction, so it's easy to understand.

> Hello!

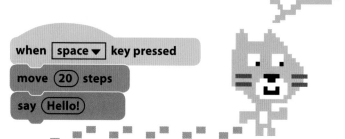

```
when  space ▼  key pressed
move  20  steps
say  Hello!
```

Working together

Games are usually made up of several sprites working together, each controlled by their own code. Code blocks make sprites move around, crash into each other, create sounds, and change color or shape.

Some sprites act as enemies to make a game more difficult.

> HELP!

EXPERT TIPS

Experimenting

Scratch is all about experimenting. Once you've built a game, it's easy to add things to it or change how it works by tinkering with the code. You can see the effect of your changes right away.

A typical Scratch project

Once you've built some code, you can click the green flag to see what it does. All the action takes place in a part of the Scratch window called the "stage." Sprites move around on the stage, often in front of a background image that helps create atmosphere.

Click here to run the program in full-screen mode.

▷ **Running a program**
Starting, or "running" a program activates the code blocks that you've built. To make the stage fill your whole computer screen, click the icon at the top right.

Starts the project   Stops the project

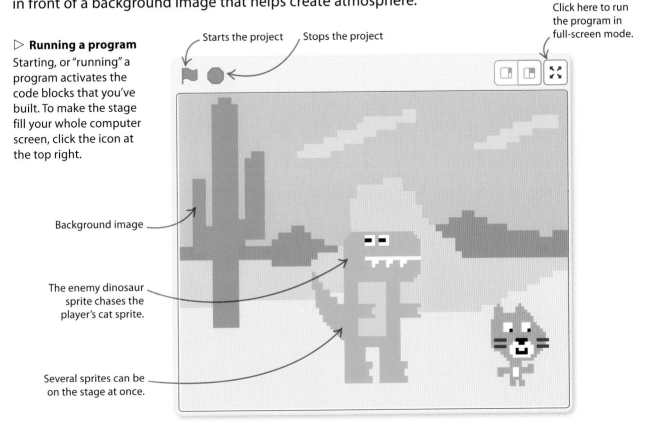

Background image

The enemy dinosaur sprite chases the player's cat sprite.

Several sprites can be on the stage at once.

▽ **Making sprites move**
In a typical game, the player moves one sprite and the other sprites are programmed to move automatically. The code below makes the dinosaur in this project chase the cat.

The "forever" block keeps the sprite moving endlessly.

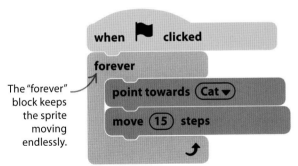

```
when ⚑ clicked
forever
    point towards (Cat ▼)
    move (15) steps
```

Getting Scratch

In order to try the projects in this book, you'll need to set up Scratch on a desktop or laptop computer. The two ways of setting up Scratch (online and offline) are shown below.

. . LINGO

Why "Scratch"?

Scratch is named after "scratching," a technique rappers and DJs use to remix music on a turntable. The Scratch programming language lets you copy other people's projects and remix them to make your own unique versions.

Online Scratch

If you have a reliable internet connection, you can run Scratch online in a browser window without downloading anything. You will need to set up a Scratch account.

1 Join Scratch

To set up the online version, visit the Scratch website at **scratch.mit.edu** and click "Join Scratch". You will need to set up an account with a username and password. Your games will stay private unless you click "Share", which will publish them on the web.

2 Sign in

After you've joined the Scratch website, click "Sign in" and enter your username and password. It's best not to use your real name as your username. Click "Create" at the top of the screen to start a new project. If you use the online version of Scratch, you can access your projects from any computer.

Offline Scratch

You can also download the Scratch program to your computer so you can use it offline. This is particularly useful if your internet connection is unreliable.

1 Install Scratch

For the offline version of Scratch, go to **scratch.mit.edu/download**. Follow the instructions on screen to download the installation files, then double-click them. After installation, a Scratch icon will appear on your desktop.

2 Launch Scratch

Double-click the icon on the desktop and Scratch will open, ready for you to begin programming. There's no need to create a user account if you use the offline version of Scratch.

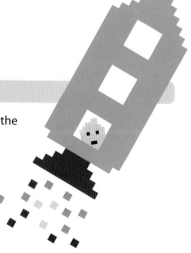

△ Operating system
The online version of Scratch works well on Windows, Ubuntu, and Mac computers. The offline version of Scratch works well on Windows and Mac computers. If your computer uses Ubuntu, try the online version instead.

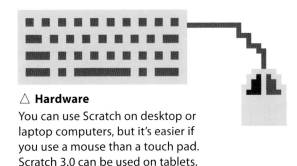

△ Hardware
You can use Scratch on desktop or laptop computers, but it's easier if you use a mouse than a touch pad. Scratch 3.0 can be used on tablets.

◁ Saving
If you use Scratch offline, remember to save from time to time. The online version saves automatically.

Old and new versions

This book is based on Scratch 3.0, the latest version at the time of writing. The projects in this book may not work with older versions of Scratch, so make sure you have 3.0.

▽ Version 2.0
In older versions of Scratch, such as Scratch 2.0, the stage is on the left and the code area is on the right.

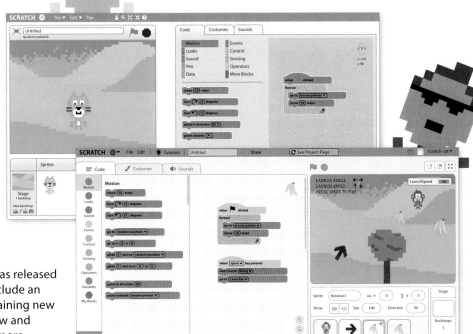

▷ Version 3.0
This version of Scratch was released in 2019. New features include an "Extension" section containing new programming blocks; new and improved sprites; and a more sophisticated sound editor.

Scratch tour

The Scratch window is divided into several different areas. Code blocks are built in the middle, while the stage on the right shows the game running.

Keep the Code tab selected to build code.

Change language

Menu options

Use the Sounds tab to add music and sound effects to games.

SCRATCH ▼   File   Edit   ☀ Tutorials   Untitled

☰ Code   ✏ Costumes   🔊 Sounds

The Costumes tab lets you change how sprites look.

Motion

Motion

move (10) steps

turn ↻ (15) degrees

turn ↺ (15) degrees

Looks

Sound

Events

Click these headings to reveal different sets of blocks.

go to (random position ▼)

go to x: (0) y: (0)

Control

glide (1) secs to (random position ▼)

Sensing

glide (1) secs to x: (0) y: (0)

Operators

point in direction (90)

Variables

point towards (mouse-pointer ▼)

My Blocks

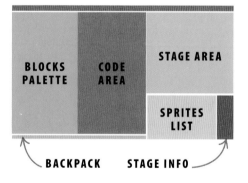

BLOCKS PALETTE | CODE AREA | STAGE AREA

SPRITES LIST

BACKPACK   STAGE INFO

△ **Scratch window**
The stage and sprites list occupy the right of the Scratch window, while code-building areas are on the left. The tabs above the code area reveal other Scratch features.

Backpack

Blocks palette
Instruction blocks for making code blocks appear on the left of the Scratch window. Drag the ones you want to use to the code area.

Backpack
Store useful code blocks, sprites, costumes, and sounds in the backpack so you can use them in other projects.

Code area
You can drag blocks into this part of the Scratch window and join them together to build some code for each sprite in your game.

The stage
When you play a game or run any other kind of project in Scratch, you see the action happening on the stage, which serves as a miniature screen. You can see changes to your code take effect immediately on the stage simply by clicking the green flag button to run the project.

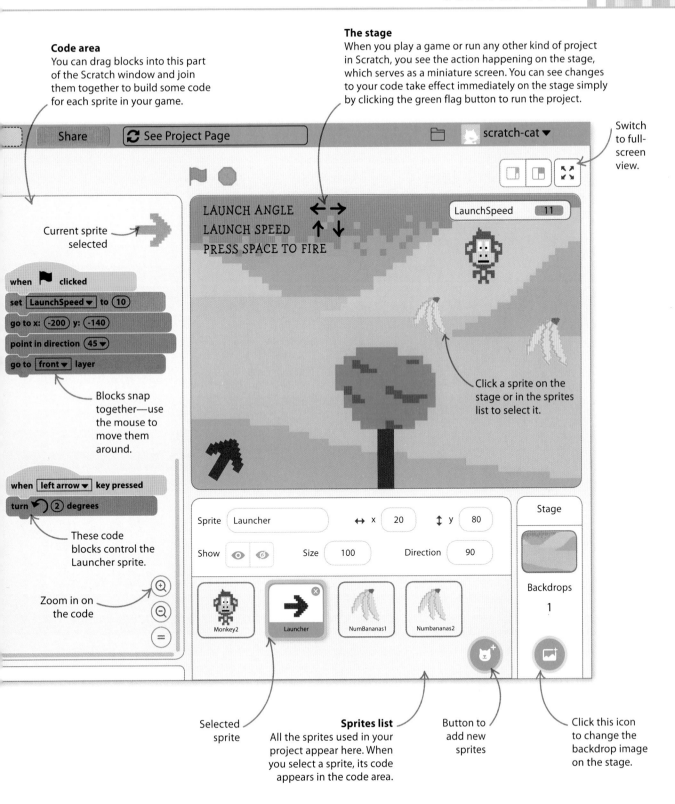

Switch to full-screen view.

Current sprite selected

```
when ⚑ clicked
set LaunchSpeed ▾ to 10
go to x: -200 y: -140
point in direction 45 ▾
go to front ▾ layer
```

LAUNCH ANGLE ← →
LAUNCH SPEED ↑ ↓
PRESS SPACE TO FIRE

LaunchSpeed   11

Blocks snap together—use the mouse to move them around.

Click a sprite on the stage or in the sprites list to select it.

```
when left arrow ▾ key pressed
turn ↻ 2 degrees
```

These code blocks control the Launcher sprite.

Zoom in on the code

Sprite Launcher   ↔ x 20   ↕ y 80
Show 👁 👁⃠   Size 100   Direction 90

Monkey2   Launcher   NumBananas1   Numbananas2

Stage

Backdrops
1

Selected sprite

Sprites list
All the sprites used in your project appear here. When you select a sprite, its code appears in the code area.

Button to add new sprites

Click this icon to change the backdrop image on the stage.

scratch-cat ▾

Star
Hunter

How to build Star Hunter

Welcome to your first Scratch game: Star Hunter, a fast-paced underwater treasure hunt. Just follow the simple steps in this chapter to build the game, and then challenge a friend to beat your score.

AIM OF THE GAME

The aim of this game is to collect as many gold stars as you can. Use the cat to collect the stars, but watch out for deadly octopuses. You'll need to move quickly to succeed. The main sprites in the game are shown below.

◁ **Cat**
Move the cat around the screen with your computer mouse—the cat sprite follows the mouse-pointer.

◁ **Octopuses**
The octopuses patrol the seas, but they swim more slowly than you. If you touch one, the game is over!

◁ **Stars**
These appear one at a time in random places. Touch a star to score a point.

Click the green flag to start a new game.

Click the stop sign to end a game.

The score shows how many stars you've collected.

Score   0

An underwater backdrop image sets the scene.

Click this icon to
make the game fill
your screen.

Collect stars
to score points.

GAME CONTROLS

Use a computer mouse
or touch pad to control
this game.

Don't touch the octopuses!
There are three octopuses, and
they move in different ways.

◁ **Under the sea**
Star Hunter is set in the deep
sea, but you can change the
backdrop to anything you like,
from outer space to a picture
of your bedroom.

Ready?
Let's code!

You play the game as a cat.
Move your computer mouse
to move the cat.

Building code

Like any Scratch program, Star Hunter is made by joining colored blocks like the pieces of a jigsaw puzzle. Each block is an instruction that tells a sprite what to do. Let's start by programming the game's main sprite: the cat.

1 Start Scratch and choose "New" from the "File" menu. You'll see a screen like the one below, with the cat sprite in place. On the left is a set of blue instruction blocks.

Clicking the buttons here reveals different sets of blocks.

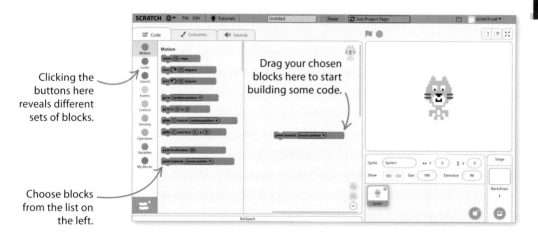

Drag your chosen blocks here to start building some code.

Choose blocks from the list on the left.

2 We'll program the cat to move wherever the player moves the computer mouse. Click on the "go to random position" block and drag it to the middle of the screen—the code area.

Some blocks include a drop-down menu.

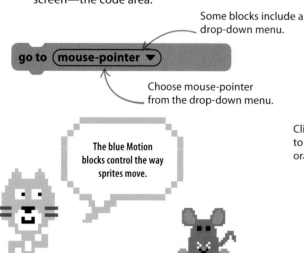

go to mouse-pointer ▼

Choose mouse-pointer from the drop-down menu.

The blue Motion blocks control the way sprites move.

3 Now select the orange Control button and look for a "forever" block.

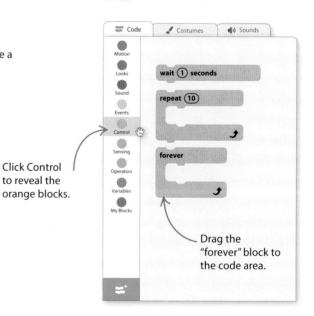

Click Control to reveal the orange blocks.

Drag the "forever" block to the code area.

4 Drag it to the right and drop it over the blue block. It will wrap around it like this:

forever
go to (mouse-pointer ▼)

5 Next, select the yellow Events button. Look for a block with a green flag. Drag it to the right and add it to the top of your code. Read through the code and think about what each block does.

when ▶ clicked
forever
go to (mouse-pointer ▼)

This block starts the game when you click the green flag.

This block makes the cat move with the player's mouse-pointer.

This block makes the block inside it repeat over and over again.

6 Now look at the top left of the stage—you'll see a green flag. Click this to run your code.

Click the green flag to play.

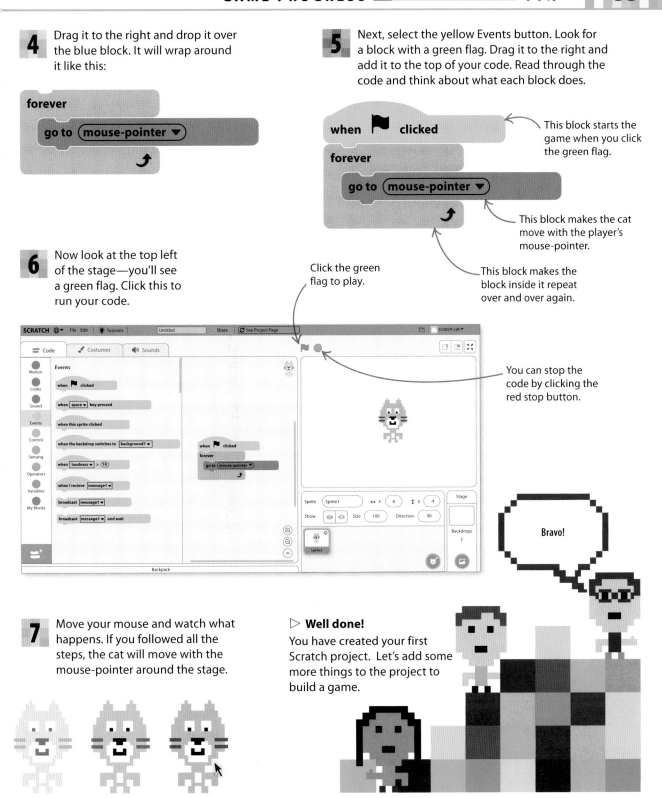

You can stop the code by clicking the red stop button.

Bravo!

7 Move your mouse and watch what happens. If you followed all the steps, the cat will move with the mouse-pointer around the stage.

▷ **Well done!**
You have created your first Scratch project. Let's add some more things to the project to build a game.

8 The cat is called "Sprite1". Let's fix that. In the sprites list, select Sprite1 (the cat). Change the name to "Cat".

Type the sprite's name here.

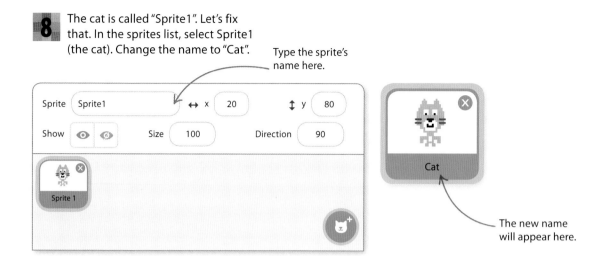

The new name will appear here.

Setting the scene

At the moment, the stage is just a boring white rectangle. Let's create some atmosphere by adding scenery and sound effects. To change the scenery, we add a "backdrop" image.

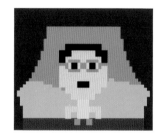

9 To the right of the sprites list is a button to add a picture from the backdrop library. Click it and look for "Underwater 2". Select the image. The backdrop will now fill the stage.

The backdrop is just decoration and doesn't affect the sprites.

Click this icon to open the backdrop library.

Choose a Backdrop

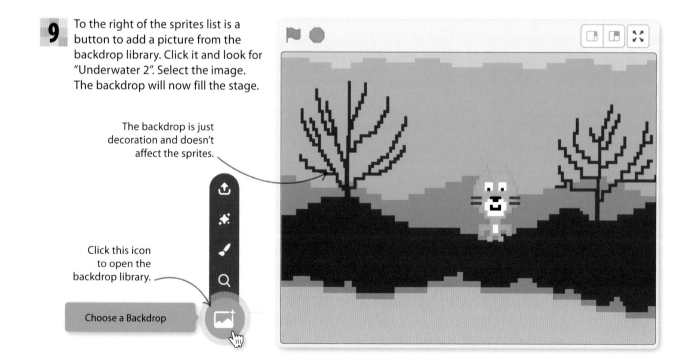

Sound effects

Now we'll add a bubbling sound to the cat sprite to make it sound like we're underwater.

10 Highlight the cat in the sprites list and then click the Sounds tab above the blocks palette. Click the speaker icon at the bottom left to choose a sound from the library.

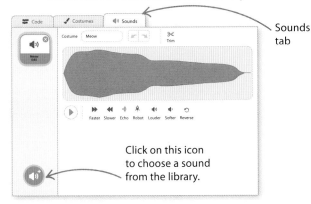

Sounds tab

Click on this icon to choose a sound from the library.

11 Look for "Bubbles" in the library. You can preview sounds by holding your mouse over the icon. To load a sound into the game, click on its icon. Now you'll see Bubbles in your list of sounds.

Delete sounds here.

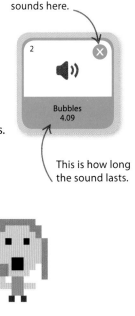

This is how long the sound lasts.

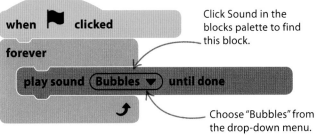

You can add sounds to the stage as well as to sprites.

12 Click the Code tab and add the following code to the cat sprite, but leave the old code in place because you need both. The new code repeats the bubbles sound. The "play sound until done" block waits for the sound to finish before letting it start again. Run the game to hear the sound effect.

Click Sound in the blocks palette to find this block.

Choose "Bubbles" from the drop-down menu.

Loops

A loop is a section of code that repeats over and over again. The "forever" block creates a loop that carries on forever, but other types of loops can repeat an action a fixed number of times. Loops are very common in almost all computer programming languages.

Blocks run from top to bottom.

The "forever" block makes the program return to the start of the block.

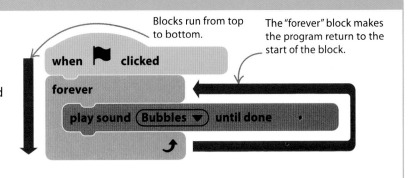

Add an enemy

The game needs an enemy to make things more interesting. Let's add an octopus with a deadly sting. The octopus will patrol the stage, moving left and right, and the player will have to keep out of its way or the game is over.

13 To add a second sprite to the project, click the icon shown below to open up the sprites library. Look for "Octopus" and select it.

Click here to open the sprites library.

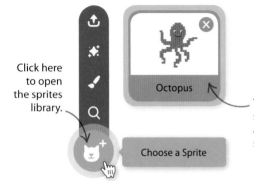

The octopus sprite will appear in your sprites list.

14 Add the following code to the octopus sprite. To find the blue blocks, click on Motion in the blocks palette. The two Motion blocks used here make the octopus move left and right across the stage.

This block runs the code when the game begins.

Motion blocks are dark blue and control the way sprites move.

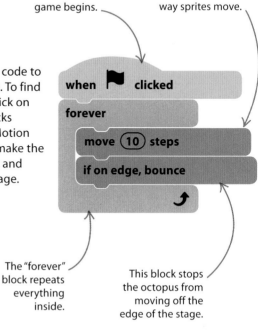

The "forever" block repeats everything inside.

This block stops the octopus from moving off the edge of the stage.

15 Now run the code. The octopus will patrol left and right, but you'll notice it's upside down half of the time. You can fix this by changing the way the sprite turns around when it changes direction. Choose the blue "set rotation style" block, and add it to the octopus's code.

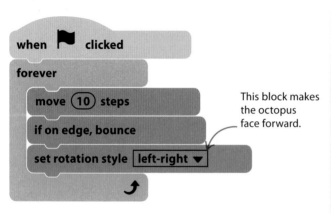

This block makes the octopus face forward.

16 The octopus should now stay right-side up and facing forward all the time. You can adjust its starting position on the screen by dragging it with the mouse.

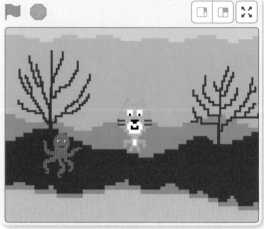

Collisions

So far the octopus and cat move through each other without anything happening. We need to add code to make them stop moving when they collide. Collision detection is very important in computer games.

17 Highlight the octopus and drag an orange "if then" block to an empty part of the code area. Now add a pale blue "touching" block to the top of the "if then" block. Click the drop-down menu and choose "Cat". This code will help the octopus detect the cat.

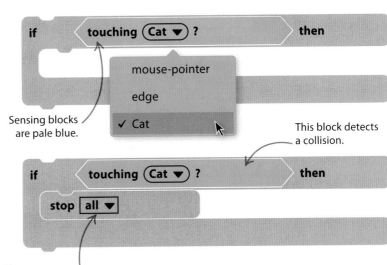

Sensing blocks are pale blue.

This block detects a collision.

18 Choose Control in the blocks palette again, and add a "stop all" block to the middle of the "if then" block. This will stop all action if the octopus is touching the cat, ending the game.

This block ends the game when the sprites collide.

19 Now add the "if then" blocks you've built to the octopus's main code, placing it carefully after the blue Motion blocks. Also, add a "wait 0.5 seconds" before the loop. Run the project and see what happens.

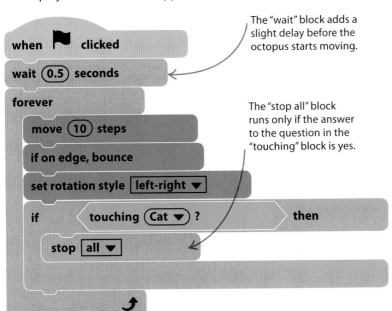

The "wait" block adds a slight delay before the octopus starts moving.

The "stop all" block runs only if the answer to the question in the "touching" block is yes.

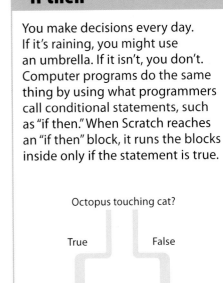

"if then"

You make decisions every day. If it's raining, you might use an umbrella. If it isn't, you don't. Computer programs do the same thing by using what programmers call conditional statements, such as "if then." When Scratch reaches an "if then" block, it runs the blocks inside only if the statement is true.

Octopus touching cat?

True　　　　False

Stop the sprites　　Keep going

More enemies

Let's add more enemies to the game, but to make things more challenging, we'll make them move in different directions. We can tell each sprite exactly which way to go by using a block that works like a compass.

20 Add a purple "set size to" block to the top of the octopus's code, after the "when clicked" block. Set the octopus's size to 35% to make the game a bit easier. Then add a blue "point in direction" block.

21 To change the octopus's direction, click on the window in the "point in direction" block and type 135 in place of 90. This will make the octopus move diagonally.

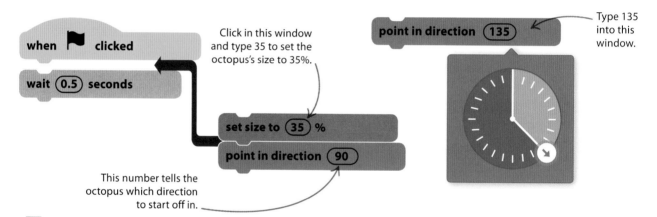

when ▸ clicked

Click in this window and type 35 to set the octopus's size to 35%.

wait (0.5) seconds

set size to (35) %

point in direction (90)

This number tells the octopus which direction to start off in.

point in direction (135)

Type 135 into this window.

▪▪▪ EXPERT TIPS

Directions

Scratch uses degrees to set direction. You can choose any number from −179° to 180°. Negative numbers point sprites left; positive numbers point them right. Use 0° to go up and 180° to go straight down.

−90° moves a sprite straight to the left.

0°

−90°   90°

180° moves a sprite straight down.

180°

22 Now we can duplicate our octopus to create more enemies. Right-click on the octopus in the sprites list (or control-click if you have a Mac) and choose "duplicate". Copies of the Octopus sprite will appear in the sprites list, named Octopus2 and Octopus3. Each will have a copy of the first octopus's code.

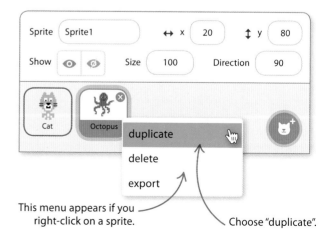

This menu appears if you right-click on a sprite.

Choose "duplicate".

23 To make the octopuses move in different directions, change the number in the "point in direction" block for each new octopus. Leave the first Octopus sprite's direction as 135, but set Octopus2 to 0 and Octopus3 to 90. Run the project and try to avoid all the enemies.

24 If it's too hard to stay alive, make the octopuses slower by lowering the number of steps in their "move" blocks to 2. Remember to change the code for all three octopus sprites.

Changing this number adjusts the octopus's speed.

```
move (2) steps
if on edge, bounce
```

25 For more variety, let's make one of the octopuses start off in a random direction. To do this, we use a green "pick random" block. This is Scratch's way of rolling a die to generate a random number. Choose Operators in the blocks palette to find the block and add it to the first octopus's code. Run the project a few times to see the octopus choose different starting directions.

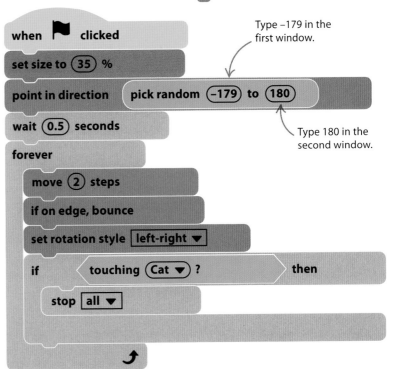

Type −179 in the first window.

Type 180 in the second window.

```
when ⚑ clicked
set size to (35) %
point in direction  pick random (−179) to (180)
wait (0.5) seconds
forever
    move (2) steps
    if on edge, bounce
    set rotation style [left-right ▼]
    if    touching (Cat ▼) ?    then
        stop [all ▼]
```

Random numbers

Why do so many games use die? Die create surprises in a game because they make different things happen to each player. A random number is one you can't predict in advance, just like the roll of a die. You can get the cat to say a random die roll using this simple code.

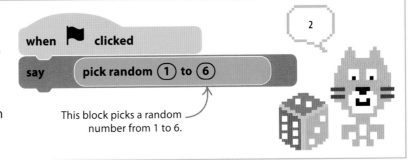

```
when ⚑ clicked
say    pick random (1) to (6)
```

This block picks a random number from 1 to 6.

2

Collecting stars

In many games, the player has to collect valuable items to win points or to stay alive. In Star Hunter, we use gold stars as underwater treasure that the player has to collect. We'll use random numbers again to make each star appear in a new place.

26 Click the "Choose a Sprite" symbol in the sprites list, and choose the Star sprite from the library.

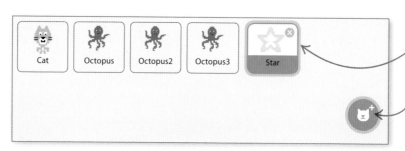

The Star sprite will appear in your sprites list.

Click this symbol to open the sprites library.

27 Add the following code to Star. This code will make the star move to a random new location whenever the cat touches it. The green blocks create random numbers called coordinates, which Scratch uses to pinpoint locations on the stage.

The "if then" block checks whether the cat is touching the star.

The "go to" block runs only if the answer to the question is yes.

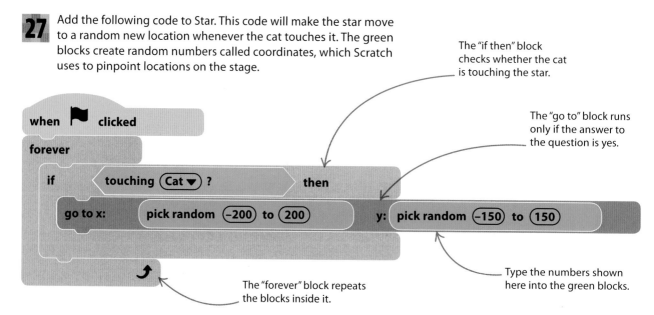

The "forever" block repeats the blocks inside it.

Type the numbers shown here into the green blocks.

28 To see the star's coordinates change when it moves, choose Motion in the blocks palette and check the boxes for "x position" and "y position". Now run the game; you'll see the star's x and y coordinates update each time the cat makes it move. Uncheck both boxes before you continue.

Star: x position   60

Star: y position   78

Using coordinates

To pinpoint a location on the stage, Scratch uses numbers called coordinates. These work just like graph coordinates, with x numbers for horizontal positions and y numbers for vertical. To find the coordinates for a spot on the stage, just count the steps across and up from the center of the stage. Positive coordinates are up or right; negative coordinates are down or left. Every spot on the stage has a unique pair of coordinates that can be used to send a sprite to that position.

The x axis is longer than the y axis and extends from –240 to 240.

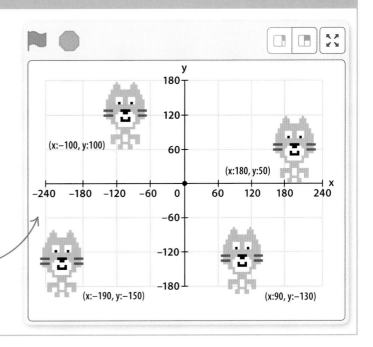

29 You can add a sound effect that plays when the cat touches a star. First make sure that the star is selected in the sprites list, and then click the Sounds tab above the blocks palette. Click the speaker symbol ◀ʲ to open the sound library and choose "Fairydust". Now add the pink "start sound" block to the star's code and choose "Fairydust" in the drop-down list.

Insert the "start sound" block into the Star's existing code, and then use the drop-down menu to choose which sound to play.

```
if    touching (Cat ▼) ?    then
    start sound (Fairydust ▼)
    go to x:    pick random (-200) to (200)    y:    pick random (-150) to (150)
```

Keeping score

Computer games often need to keep track of vital statistics, such as the player's score or health. We call these changing numbers "variables." To keep track of the player's score in Star Hunter, we'll create a variable that counts the number of stars the player has collected.

30 With any sprite selected, choose Variables in the blocks palette. Click on the button "Make a Variable".

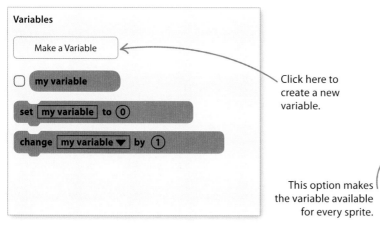

Click here to create a new variable.

This option makes the variable available for every sprite.

31 A pop-up box appears asking you to give your variable a name. Type "Score" in the box. Make sure the option "For all sprites" is selected and hit "OK".

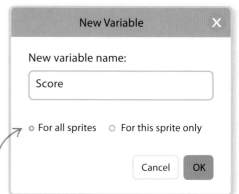

32 You'll see a new set of blocks appear, including one for the score. Make sure the box next to it is checked to make the score appear on the stage.

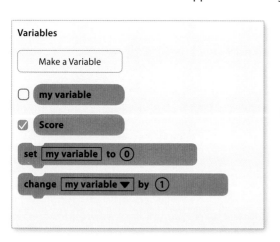

You can use the mouse to move the score display.

33 The score counter will appear in the top left of the stage, but you can drag it anywhere you like.

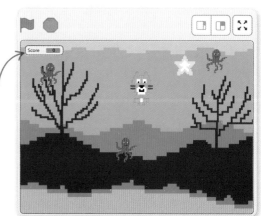

34 We want the score to start at 0 and increase by 1 each time the cat touches a star. Select the star sprite, and add the two orange Variables blocks below to its code.

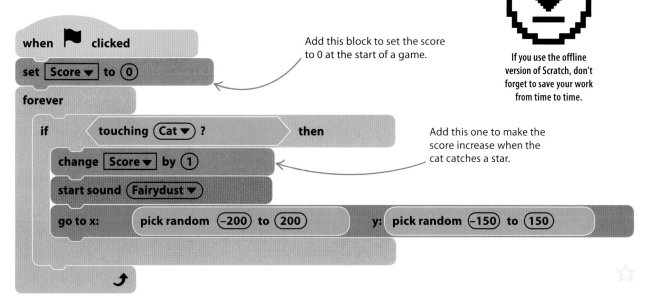

Add this block to set the score to 0 at the start of a game.

Add this one to make the score increase when the cat catches a star.

If you use the offline version of Scratch, don't forget to save your work from time to time.

35 Now click the green flag to run the code and see what happens when the cat collects each star. See if you can collect 20 stars without bumping into an octopus.

EXPERT TIPS

Variables

A variable works like a box that you can store information in, such as a number that can change. In math, we use letters for variables, such as x and y. In computer programming, we give variables names such as "Score" and use them for storing not just numbers but any kind of information. Try to choose a name that tells you what the variable is for, such as "Speed" or "Score." Most computer languages won't let you put spaces in the names of variables, so a good tip is to combine words. Instead of using "dog speed," for instance, type "DogSpeed."

Hey, I'm X years old!

Big deal, I'm Y years old!

Better enemies

Now that we have a working game, we can test it and experiment with changes that make it easier, harder, or—most important—more fun. One way to make the game more interesting is to make the three octopuses do different things.

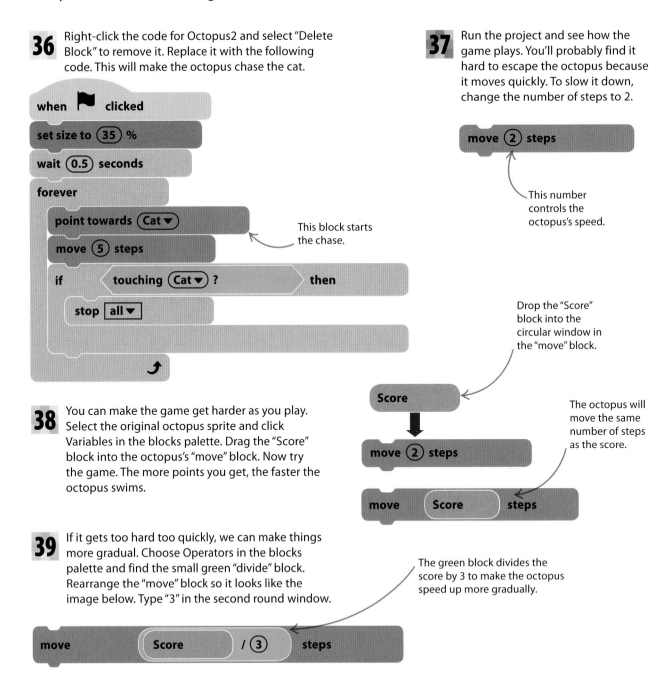

36 Right-click the code for Octopus2 and select "Delete Block" to remove it. Replace it with the following code. This will make the octopus chase the cat.

when ⚑ clicked

set size to (35) %

wait (0.5) seconds

forever

    point towards (Cat ▼)

    move (5) steps

    if ⟨ touching (Cat ▼) ? ⟩ then

        stop [all ▼]

This block starts the chase.

37 Run the project and see how the game plays. You'll probably find it hard to escape the octopus because it moves quickly. To slow it down, change the number of steps to 2.

move (2) steps

This number controls the octopus's speed.

38 You can make the game get harder as you play. Select the original octopus sprite and click Variables in the blocks palette. Drag the "Score" block into the octopus's "move" block. Now try the game. The more points you get, the faster the octopus swims.

Drop the "Score" block into the circular window in the "move" block.

Score

move (2) steps

move (Score) steps

The octopus will move the same number of steps as the score.

39 If it gets too hard too quickly, we can make things more gradual. Choose Operators in the blocks palette and find the small green "divide" block. Rearrange the "move" block so it looks like the image below. Type "3" in the second round window.

The green block divides the score by 3 to make the octopus speed up more gradually.

move (Score / 3) steps

40 Now we'll make Octopus3 patrol in a regular pattern. To do this, we'll use a new Motion block that makes it glide smoothly from point to point instead of moving in steps. Replace the code for Octopus3 with the following two blocks of code. These run at the same time, one checking for collisions and the other moving the octopus around its patrol route.

The two blocks of code are separate in the code area.

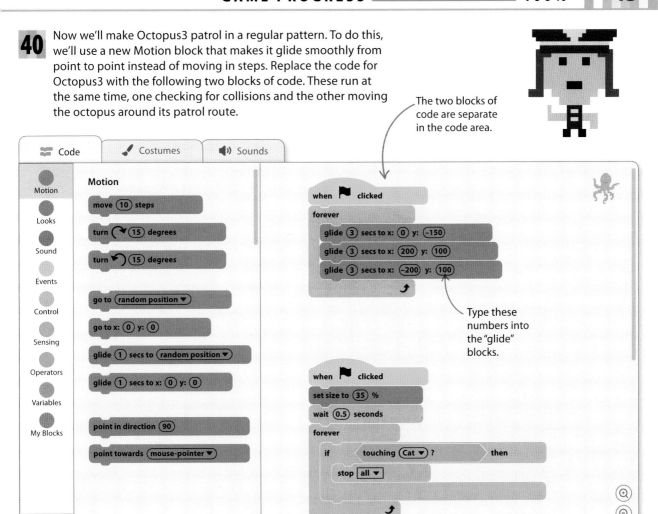

Type these numbers into the "glide" blocks.

41 Now run the project and watch Octopus3. It should swim in a repeating triangle pattern.

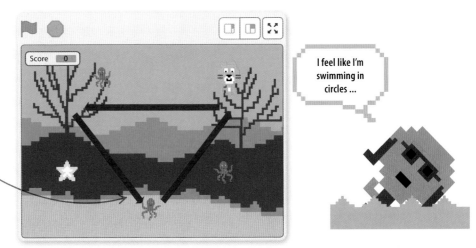

To change the shape of the triangle, try different numbers in the "glide" blocks.

I feel like I'm swimming in circles ...

Hacks and tweaks

You've built a fun game, but that's just the beginning. Scratch makes it easy to change and adapt games as much as you want. You might find bugs that need fixing, or you might want to make the game harder or easier. Here are some suggestions to get you started.

▽ **Debug Octopus2**

If Octopus2 ends up in the top-right corner at the end of a game, it can trap the player in the next game and end it too quickly. This is a bug. To fix it, you could drag the octopus away from the corner before starting, but it's better to use code that moves it automatically. Insert a "go to" block at the start of the code for Octopus2 to send it to the center of the stage.

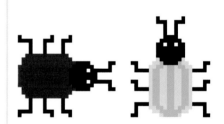

LINGO

Bugs

A bug is an error in a program. The first computers made mistakes when real insects, or bugs, got in their circuits. The name stuck. Today, programmers often spend as much time finding and fixing bugs as they do writing code in the first place.

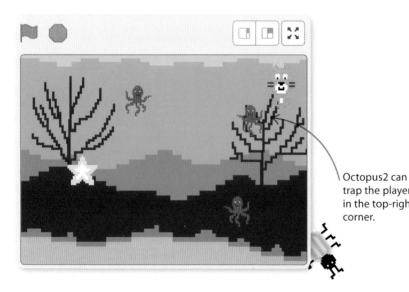

Octopus2 can trap the player in the top-right corner.

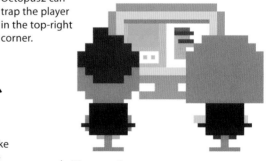

Add this block to make Octopus2 start in the center of the stage.

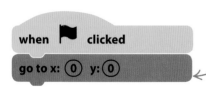

△ **Fine-tuning**

The best games have been carefully tested to make sure they play well. Test every change you make, and get friends to play your games to see how well they work.

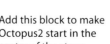

▽ **Different colors**

Make your octopuses different colors by using the "set color" block from the Looks section. Place it under the "set size" block at the start of the code.

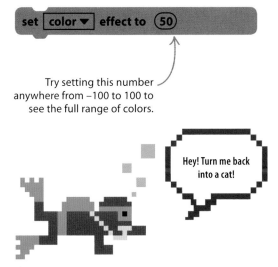

set color ▼ effect to (50)

Try setting this number anywhere from −100 to 100 to see the full range of colors.

Hey! Turn me back into a cat!

△ **Scuba diver**

To make the underwater theme more convincing, replace the cat with a diver. Click on the cat in the sprites list and then open the Costumes tab. Click on the sprite symbol 🐱 to open the library, and find a diver costume.

▽ **Flashing colors**

You can make an octopus change color continually to create a flashing effect. Add the code below to any octopus. Try experimenting with different numbers in the "change color" block.

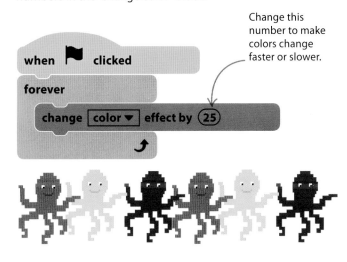

Change this number to make colors change faster or slower.

when 🚩 clicked

forever

change color ▼ effect by (25)

▽ **Play with size**

You can change how easy the game is by adjusting the size of the sprites. Change the number in the octopuses' blue "move" blocks to alter their speed. Change the purple "set size" blocks to make sprites larger or smaller. Fine-tune the numbers until the game is just hard enough to be fun.

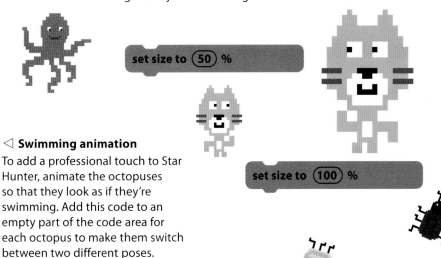

set size to (50) %

set size to (100) %

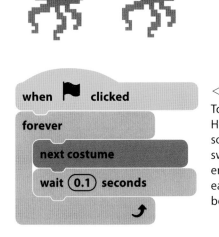

when 🚩 clicked

forever

next costume

wait (0.1) seconds

◁ **Swimming animation**

To add a professional touch to Star Hunter, animate the octopuses so that they look as if they're swimming. Add this code to an empty part of the code area for each octopus to make them switch between two different poses.

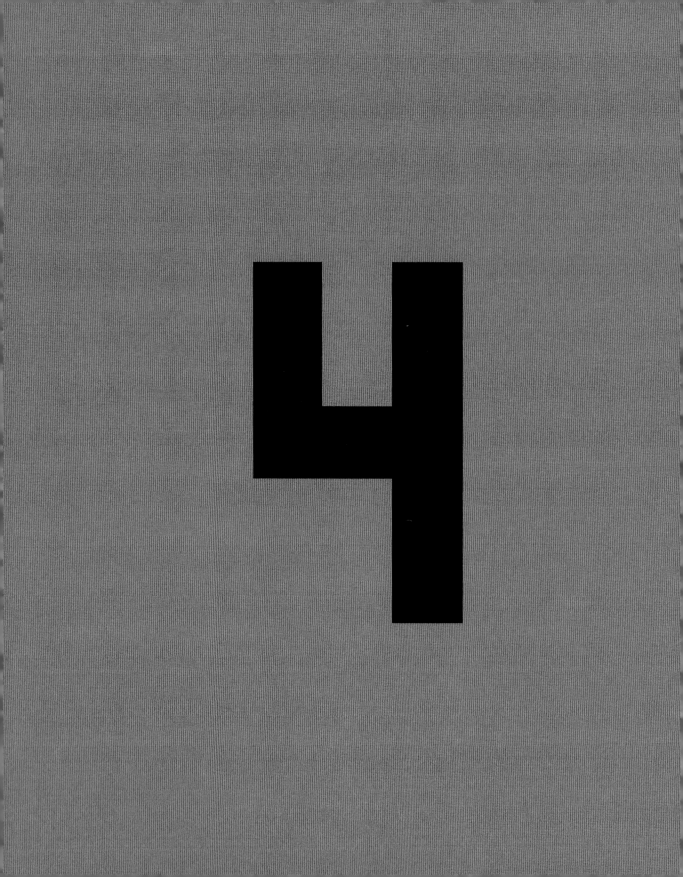

Cheese Chase

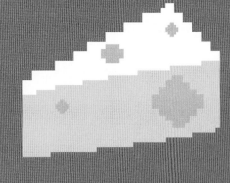

How to build Cheese Chase

Some of the world's first and most popular computer games were maze games. In a maze game, quick thinking is essential as you race around tight corners, avoiding monsters and collecting treats.

AIM OF THE GAME

Mimi the mouse is hungry and stuck in a maze. Help her find the cheese, but avoid the evil beetles. And watch out for ghosts—the maze is haunted!

◁ **Mimi**
You play the game as the mouse. Use the arrow keys on your keyboard to make her run up, down, left, or right.

◁ **Beetles**
Beetles scuttle along the edges and make random turns when they hit a wall.

◁ **Ghosts**
Ghosts can float through walls. They can appear anywhere without warning and then disappear.

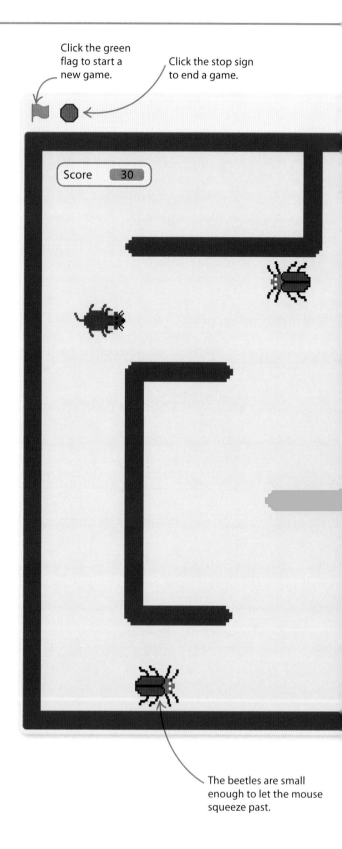

Click the green flag to start a new game.

Click the stop sign to end a game.

Score   30

The beetles are small enough to let the mouse squeeze past.

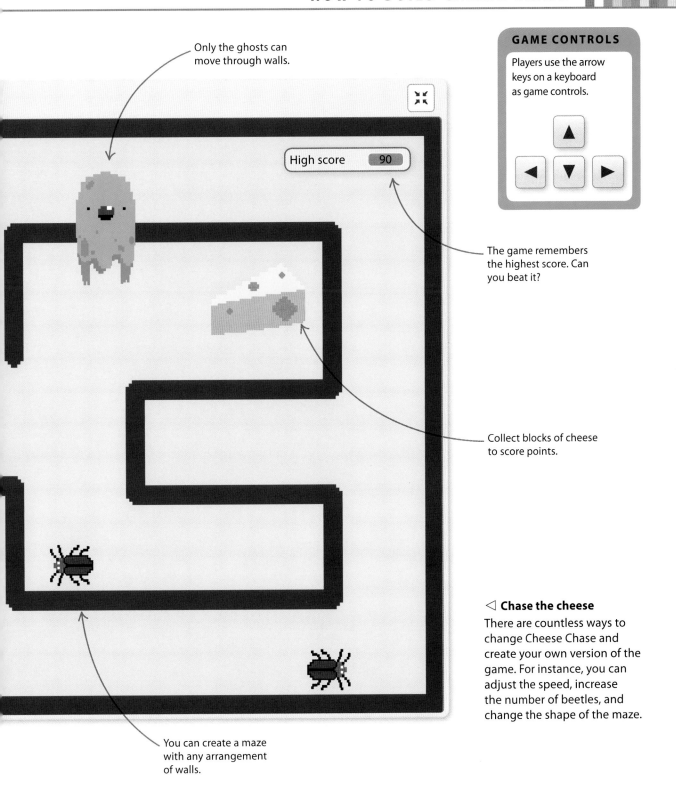

Only the ghosts can move through walls.

High score   90

Collect blocks of cheese to score points.

You can create a maze with any arrangement of walls.

GAME CONTROLS

Players use the arrow keys on a keyboard as game controls.

The game remembers the highest score. Can you beat it?

◁ **Chase the cheese**
There are countless ways to change Cheese Chase and create your own version of the game. For instance, you can adjust the speed, increase the number of beetles, and change the shape of the maze.

Keyboard control

Many games let the player use the keyboard to control the action. In Cheese Chase, the player uses the arrow keys on the keyboard to move Mimi the mouse around the stage. Start by creating some keyboard control code for Mimi.

1 Start Scratch and choose "New" from the "File" menu. Delete the cat by right-clicking and selecting "delete". If you use a Mac computer, instead of right-clicking, you can hold down the control key and click.

2 Click the "Choose a Sprite" symbol, and look through the sprites library for Mouse1. Click on it. The mouse should now be on the stage and in the sprites list.

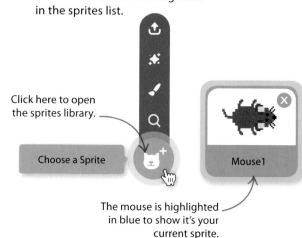

Click here to open the sprites library.

The mouse is highlighted in blue to show it's your current sprite.

3 Add this code to the mouse to move the sprite up the stage using the up arrow key. To find the different-colored blocks, remember to click the different options in the Code tab. Read through the code carefully and think about what it does. Run the code by clicking the green flag. You should be able to move the Mouse sprite up the stage using the up arrow key.

Everything inside the "forever" loop repeats endlessly.

Click the triangle and select "up arrow" to choose the correct keyboard key.

```
when [flag] clicked
forever
    if < key (up arrow ▼) pressed? > then
        point in direction (0)
        move (5) steps
```

This block makes the mouse face upward.

The blocks inside the "if then" block run only when the answer to the question is yes.

This block makes the mouse move.

4 To make the other arrow keys work, add three more "if then" blocks like the first one, but choose a different arrow key and direction for each one. To move right, select the right arrow key and set the direction to 90. For down, set it to 180. For left, set it to –90. Read through the finished code to make sure you understand it.

Each "if then" block should be inside the "forever" loop but not inside any of the other "if then" blocks.

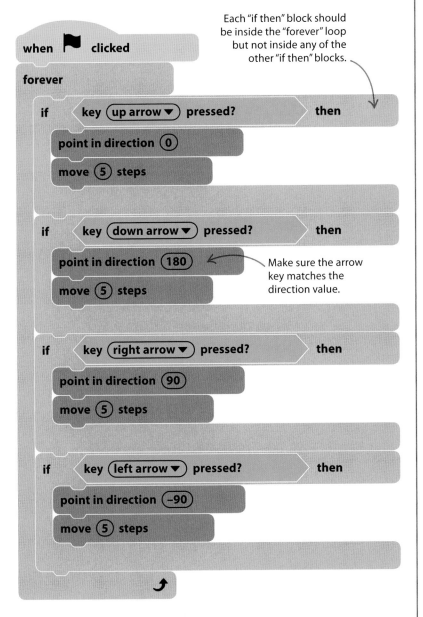

Make sure the arrow key matches the direction value.

Controllers

In Cheese Chase, we use the arrow keys to control the game, and in Star Hunter, we used the mouse. Other computer games use very different types of controllers.

▷ **Console controller**
Console controllers usually have two small joysticks controlled with your thumbs, along with a range of other buttons. They are ideal for complex games that need a lot of different controls.

▷ **Dance mats**
You control the game by stepping on giant keys. Dance mats are good for games involving physical activity, but they don't give fine control.

▷ **Motion sensor**
These controllers detect movement, which makes them ideal for sports games where you swing your arms to use a racquet or bat, for example.

▷ **Camera**
Special cameras in some game consoles allow the player to use body movements to control the game.

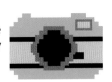

5 Now click the green flag to run the code. You should be able to move the mouse in all directions around the stage using the arrow keys. If it's not working, go back and check all the steps.

Using the paint editor

Cheese Chase now has its mouse heroine, and she's hungry, but there's no cheese yet for her to chase. The sprites library in Scratch doesn't include a picture of cheese, so you'll need to make one yourself. You can do this with Scratch's paint editor.

My cheese piece is a masterpiece!

6 Create a blank sprite by clicking the small paintbrush symbol in the sprites menu. This will open Scratch's paint editor in a screen like the one below. Make sure "Convert to Bitmap" is selected at the bottom.

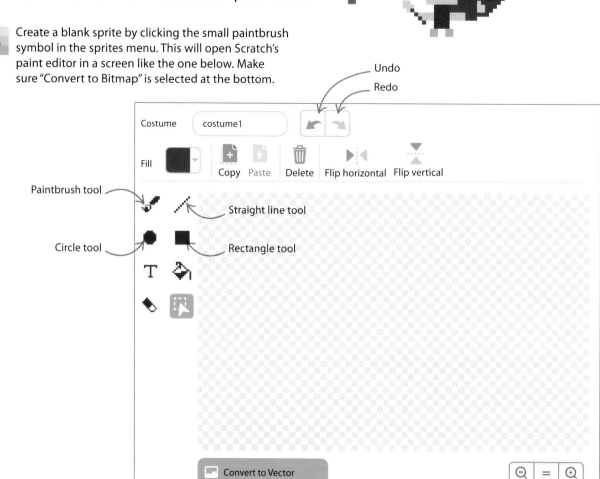

Undo
Redo

Costume   costume1

Fill

Copy   Paste   Delete   Flip horizontal   Flip vertical

Paintbrush tool
Straight line tool

Circle tool
Rectangle tool

Convert to Vector

7 Now draw the cheese. Use the paintbrush tool, and choose black from the color palette in the "Fill" menu. Draw the outline of the cheese. If you want perfectly straight lines, use the line tool. Your cheese drawing might be too big at first, but you can make it smaller later.

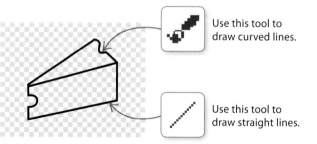

Use this tool to draw curved lines.

Use this tool to draw straight lines.

8 If you like, use the circle tool to draw holes in the cheese. Make the circle an outline instead of a solid circle by choosing the outline option at the bottom.

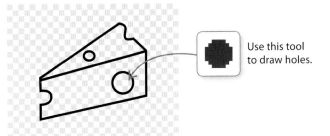

Use this tool to draw holes.

9 To add color, choose yellow and use the fill tool to fill in the cheese. If your color spills out and fills the whole background, click on the "undo" button. Make sure your lines don't have any gaps, and then try again. The cheese is now ready to be added to the game.

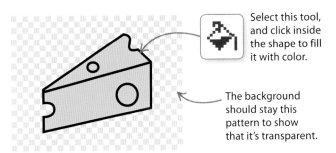

Select this tool, and click inside the shape to fill it with color.

The background should stay this pattern to show that it's transparent.

10 To keep score, we need to create a variable called "Score". Choose Variables in the blocks palette, and click on "Make a Variable". Type the word "Score" in the pop-up box. Check the box beside this new variable, and the score counter will now appear on the stage.

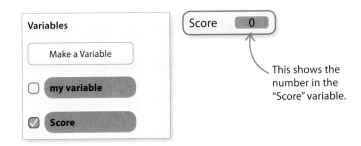

Variables

Make a Variable

◯ my variable

☑ Score

Score   0

This shows the number in the "Score" variable.

11 Now add some code to make the cheese appear in a random location. When the mouse touches it, there will be a "pop" noise, the player will score 10 points, and the cheese will move to a new location. Run the code and try catching the cheese. It should be easy—but that's because you haven't added enemies yet ...

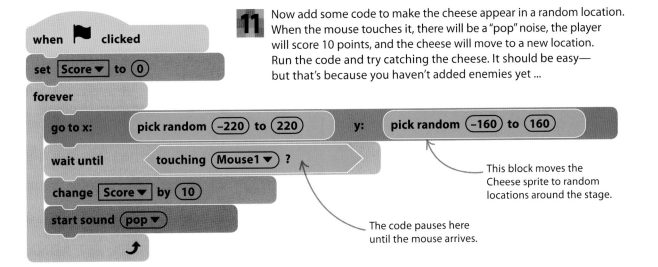

```
when 🚩 clicked
set Score ▼ to 0
forever
  go to x: pick random -220 to 220  y: pick random -160 to 160
  wait until  touching Mouse1 ▼ ?
  change Score ▼ by 10
  start sound pop ▼
```

This block moves the Cheese sprite to random locations around the stage.

The code pauses here until the mouse arrives.

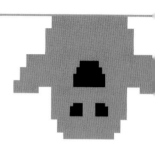

Getting spooky

Adding our first enemy to the project will make Cheese Chase into a real game. A ghost is a good first enemy for this game because it can float through walls, so you won't need to change the ghost's code when we add the maze.

12 Click the "Choose a Sprite" symbol, and select a ghost sprite from the sprites library. Click "OK" to add it to the project.

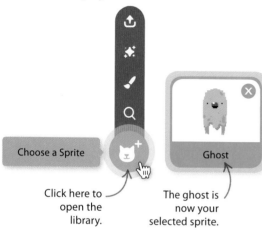

Choose a Sprite

Click here to open the library.

Ghost

The ghost is now your selected sprite.

13 Add the following code to the ghost to make it chase the mouse. If it touches the mouse, the game will end. You might recognize most of this code from Star Hunter.

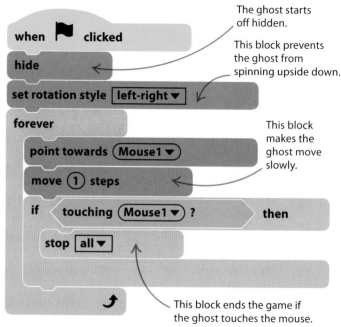

The ghost starts off hidden.

This block prevents the ghost from spinning upside down.

This block makes the ghost move slowly.

This block ends the game if the ghost touches the mouse.

Starts a new block of code. Ghost will now have two code blocks.

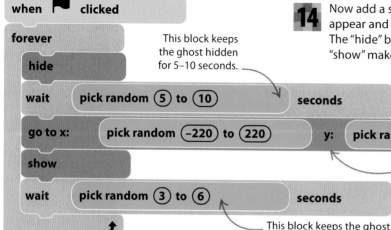

This block keeps the ghost hidden for 5–10 seconds.

14 Now add a separate block of code to make the ghost appear and disappear for random amounts of time. The "hide" block makes the sprite disappear, and "show" makes it appear again.

This block makes the ghost appear in a random place on the stage.

This block keeps the ghost on screen for 3–6 seconds.

15 Next, add music to the game. We usually add music to the stage instead of a sprite. Click the stage area on the right of the sprites list to highlight it in blue. Click the Code tab, and add the following code to play a sound over and over. Click "Sound" in the blocks palette to find the "play sound until done" block.

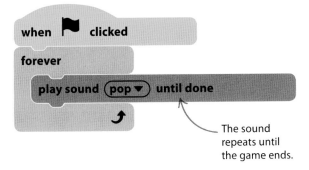

The sound repeats until the game ends.

16 Now click the Sounds tab above the blocks palette. Click the speaker symbol to open the sound library. Select the category "Loops" on the right, and then choose the music "Xylo1". Repeat the process to load "Dance Celebrate" into the game, too.

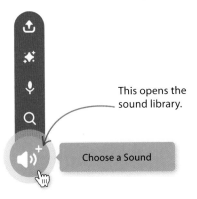

This opens the sound library.

17 Return to the Code tab, and change the selected sound from "pop" to "Xylo1". Run the game and think about how it feels to play. Next try the sound "Dance Celebrate". Which one is better?

Click the triangle to choose the sound.

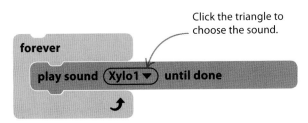

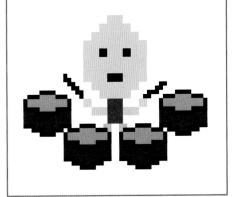
You never know where I'll appear next!

Making mazes

Mimi the mouse can run anywhere she likes on the stage. Put a stop to that by adding a maze. The maze will make it difficult for her to move from one place to another, adding an extra challenge to Cheese Chase.

ENTER MAZE HERE

18 The maze will be a sprite, not a backdrop, because that makes it easier to detect when another sprite touches it. Draw it in Scratch's paint editor. Click on the paintbrush symbol in the sprites menu, and rename the sprite "Maze".

Rename this sprite "Maze".

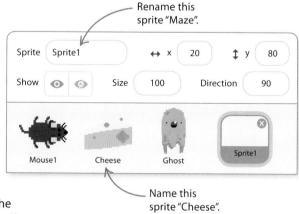

| Sprite | Sprite1 | ↔ x | 20 | ↕ y | 80 |

| Show | 👁 👁 | Size | 100 | Direction | 90 |

Mouse1   Cheese   Ghost   Sprite1

Name this sprite "Cheese".

19 Now you can start using the paint editor. Click the "Convert to Bitmap" button to change the mode. Choose the line tool, and set the line width to 20. Then pick a dark color for the maze walls.

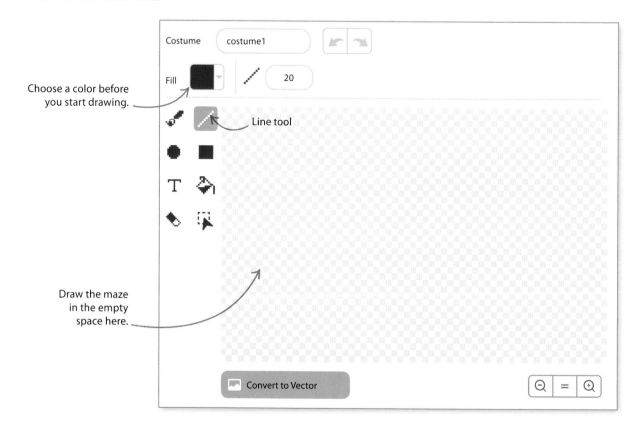

| Costume | costume1 |

Choose a color before you start drawing.

Fill

20

Line tool

Draw the maze in the empty space here.

Convert to Vector

20 Now draw the maze. Start by drawing the outside of the maze at the outer edge of the checkered drawing area. Hold down the shift key on your keyboard to make sure lines are perfectly vertical or horizontal. Then add the inside walls.

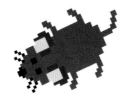

| Costume | costume1 | 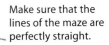 |

Fill | 20

Make sure that the lines of the maze are perfectly straight.

Convert to Vector

Q = Q

21 Finally, we need to add some code to make sure the maze is always in the center of the stage so it's fully visible. With the Maze sprite selected, click on the Code tab and add the following code.

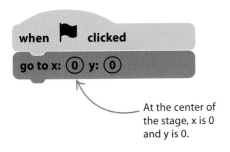

```
when 🏳 clicked
go to x: 0 y: 0
```

At the center of the stage, x is 0 and y is 0.

22 Run the project. You'll find that Mimi can run through walls, but don't worry because we'll fix that later.

23 Mimi, the ghost, and the cheese are all too big for the maze, so we need to shrink them. Add the following blocks at the beginning of Mimi's code, before the "forever" block, and fill in the numbers below.

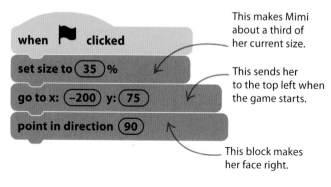

This makes Mimi about a third of her current size.

This sends her to the top left when the game starts.

This block makes her face right.

24 Now add a purple "set size to" block to the ghost's main code. Set the size to 35 percent. Add a "set size to" block to the Cheese sprite, too, and adjust the percentage until the cheese is about twice the size of Mimi.

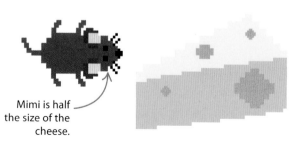

Mimi is half the size of the cheese.

25 You might need to fine-tune your Maze costume to make sure Mimi can fit through all the passages with enough room to pass her enemies (which we're going to add later). To alter the maze, select the Maze sprite, and click the Costumes tab. Use the eraser tool ✎ to remove walls or the selection tool ⬚ to move them.

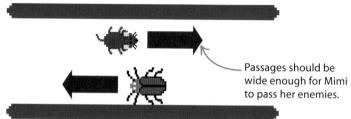

Passages should be wide enough for Mimi to pass her enemies.

26 If you use the eraser, be careful not to leave any flecks of paint behind because Mimi will stop if she hits them. Check the corners of the maze for bumps that Mimi might get stuck on and remove them.

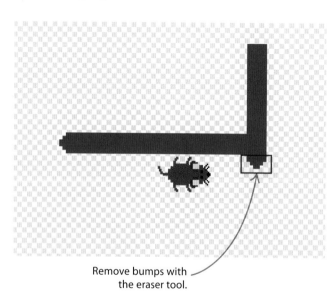

Remove bumps with the eraser tool.

27 Add a background color to the game by painting a backdrop, not the Maze sprite. At the bottom right of the screen, click the paintbrush symbol in the stage info area. This opens the paint editor. Make sure "Convert to Bitmap" is selected at the bottom.

Click here to paint the backdrop.

Choose a Backdrop

28 Choose a color, select the fill tool ◈, and then click on the backdrop to fill it with color.

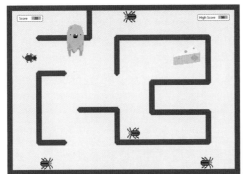

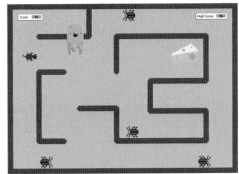

Try different colors to see which one looks best in the maze.

⋅ ⋅ ■ GAME DESIGN

Space in games

How the obstacles in a game are laid out has a big effect on how you play. A maze is the perfect obstacle to demonstrate this.

Walls restrict movement.

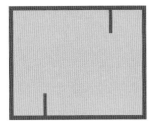

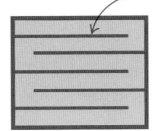

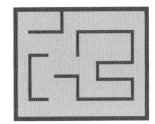

△ **Open space**
The player can move in any direction most of the time. A game like this needs fast-moving enemies or lots of enemies to make it challenging.

△ **Closed-in space**
The player is forced to move in a very limited way. Just one enemy patrolling the corridors of this maze would make life hard. The player has to think ahead to avoid getting trapped.

△ **Balanced space**
This is what the maze in Cheese Chase is designed to be. It limits the player's movement enough to make the game interesting but allows some freedom.

Mousetrap

Mimi can currently run straight through the walls of the maze like a ghost, but we want her to stay trapped inside the passages. Time to change her code.

Uh oh!

29 Select Mimi and drag the following blocks to an empty part of the code area. This set of blocks will make Mimi reverse if she runs into a wall.

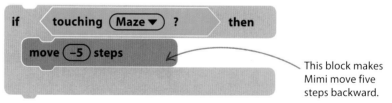

This block makes Mimi move five steps backward.

30 Insert the blocks four times into Mimi's main code. To make copies, right-click (or control-click if you use a Mac) on the new blocks, and select "duplicate". Place the duplicates after each "move 5 steps" block.

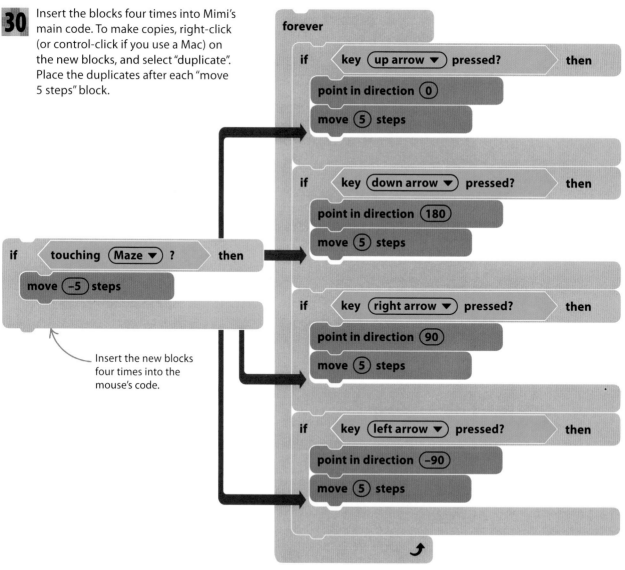

Insert the new blocks four times into the mouse's code.

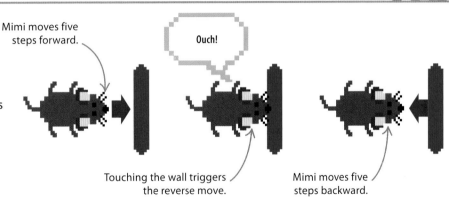

Mimi moves five
steps forward.

Ouch!

Touching the wall triggers
the reverse move.

Mimi moves five
steps backward.

▷ How does it work?

You might wonder why Mimi has to move five steps backward. The reason is that she normally moves forward five steps at a time. The backward move reverses the forward one, making her stand still. This happens so quickly that you don't see her reverse.

31 If Mimi's tail or paws touch a wall when she turns around, she can get stuck. We can fix this bug by making some changes to Mimi's costume in the paint editor.

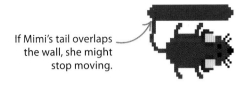

If Mimi's tail overlaps
the wall, she might
stop moving.

32 Select Mouse1 in the sprites list, and click the Costumes tab above the blocks palette. Choose "Convert to Bitmap" at the bottom, and then use the eraser tool to trim Mimi's tail.

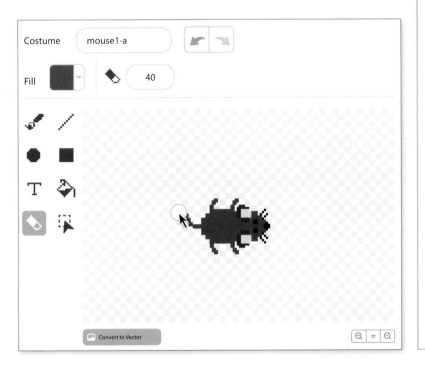

Costume   mouse1-a   ↶ ↷

Fill   ▨ ▾   ◈ 40

Convert to Vector   ⊖ = ⊕

EXPERT TIPS
Bounding boxes

One of the big challenges that game programmers face is detecting when sprites with complicated shapes collide. Even in simple 2-D games, collision detection can cause problems, such as sprites getting stuck or solid objects merging. A common solution is to use "bounding boxes"—invisible rectangles or circles that surround the sprite. When these simple shapes intersect, a collision is detected. In 3-D games, spheres or 3-D boxes can do the same job.

Beetle mania

Now for Mimi's main enemies: a small army of evil beetles that scurry around inside the maze. If she bumps into one, the game ends.

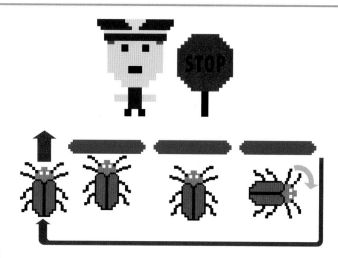

33 To make the beetles move automatically, you need to create a sequence of steps for them to follow. Programmers call this an algorithm. Our algorithm will tell each beetle to move forward until it hits a wall. Then it will stop, turn, and move forward again.

34 Click the "Choose a Sprite" symbol, and select the Beetle sprite from the library.

The beetle is now your selected sprite.

Beetle

35 Add the following code to set the beetle's size, location, and direction. It uses a "forever" loop to move the beetle and an "if then" block to make it stop and turn right whenever it hits a wall.

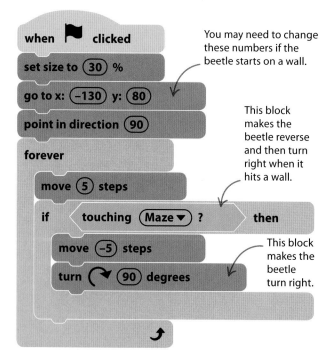

when ⚑ clicked

set size to (30) %

go to x: (−130) y: (80)

point in direction (90)

forever

  move (5) steps

  if touching (Maze ▾) ? then

    move (−5) steps

    turn ↻ (90) degrees

You may need to change these numbers if the beetle starts on a wall.

This block makes the beetle reverse and then turn right when it hits a wall.

This block makes the beetle turn right.

36 Run the code. You might notice a glitch: the beetle always turns right and ends up going around in loops. We need to change the code so that the beetle turns left or right at random. To make a random choice, use a "pick random" block. Drag it to an empty part of the code area and set the second number to 2.

Type "2" here

pick random (1) to (2)

1

Click the "pick random" block. You'll see "1" or "2" appear in a speech bubble at random.

37 Now drag the "pick random" block into the first window of an "equal to" block. Then drag the "equal to" block into an "if then else" block.

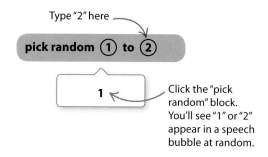

if ⬡ then

else

This is an "equal to" block.

◯ = (1)

Type "1" in this window.

pick random (1) to (2)

38 Add two "turn 90 degrees" blocks to make the beetle turn left or right. Read through the code carefully and see if you can figure out how it works.

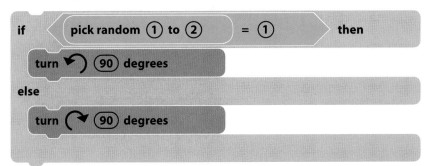

```
if   pick random 1 to 2  = 1      then
    turn ↶ 90 degrees
else
    turn ↷ 90 degrees
```

39 Remove the "turn 90 degrees" block from the beetle's original code, and put the "if then else" block in its place, as below. Run the project and watch what happens. Make sure there's enough room for Mimi to squeeze past the beetle. If not, adjust the maze in the paint editor.

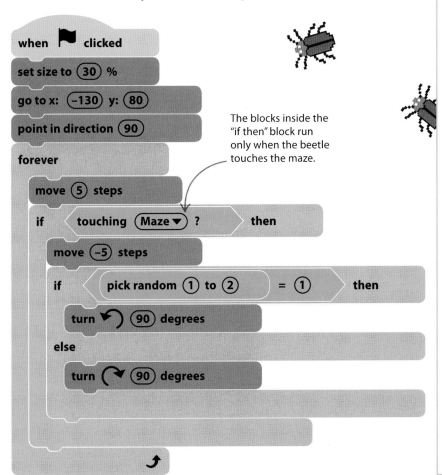

```
when ⚑ clicked
set size to 30 %
go to x: -130 y: 80
point in direction 90
forever
    move 5 steps
    if   touching Maze ▼ ?    then
        move -5 steps
        if   pick random 1 to 2  = 1    then
            turn ↶ 90 degrees
        else
            turn ↷ 90 degrees
```

The blocks inside the "if then" block run only when the beetle touches the maze.

⸬⸬ EXPERT TIPS

if then else

The "if then else" block is just like an "if then" but with an extra trick. A normal "if then" asks a question and runs the blocks inside only if the answer is yes. The "if then else" block can hold two groups of blocks: one to run if the answer is yes and another if the answer is no. The words "if," "then," and "else" are used in nearly all computer languages to make decisions between two options.

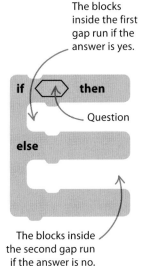

The blocks inside the first gap run if the answer is yes.

```
if  ◇  then

    — Question

else

```

The blocks inside the second gap run if the answer is no.

Sending messages

The next step is to make the beetle end the game if Mimi bumps into it. Instead of using another "touching" block in Mimi's code, you can use a message. Scratch lets you send messages between sprites to trigger code blocks. The beetle will send a message to Mimi that stops her code.

I have a message for you …

40 Add the "if then" blocks shown below to the beetle's code. The new blocks check whether the beetle is touching Mimi, and, if it is, they send a message. Select "Mouse1" in the "touching" block.

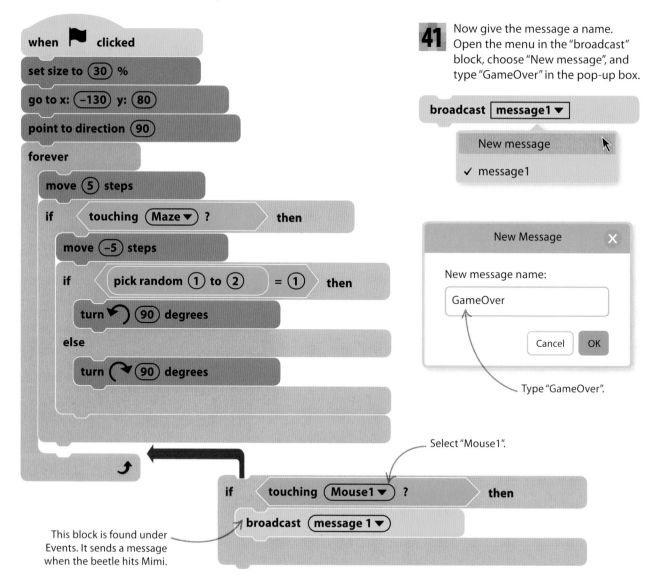

41 Now give the message a name. Open the menu in the "broadcast" block, choose "New message", and type "GameOver" in the pop-up box.

broadcast message1 ▼

New message

✓ message1

New Message ✕

New message name:

GameOver

Cancel OK

Type "GameOver".

Select "Mouse1".

when 🏴 clicked

set size to (30) %

go to x: (-130) y: (80)

point to direction (90)

forever

move (5) steps

if touching (Maze ▼) ? then

move (-5) steps

if pick random (1) to (2) = (1) then

turn ↺ (90) degrees

else

turn ↻ (90) degrees

if touching (Mouse1 ▼) ? then

broadcast (message 1 ▼)

This block is found under Events. It sends a message when the beetle hits Mimi.

42 Now add some extra code to Mimi to receive the message. Drag the following blocks to an empty part of her code area. Try the game out. Mimi should stop moving when she touches the beetle, but the beetle will continue to move. Later, we'll use a message to show a GAME OVER! sign as well.

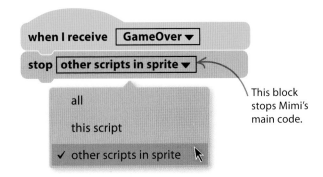

This block stops Mimi's main code.

43 The game needs more beetles. Copy the Beetle sprite by right-clicking on it (use control-click if you work on a Mac) and then choosing "duplicate". Make three new beetles. These will all have the same code. See what happens when you run the project.

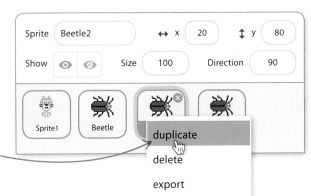

Select "duplicate" to create new beetles.

44 You'll need to change the numbers in the "go to" blocks for each new beetle so they don't all start in the same place. Starting in different corners works quite well. Experiment!

Beetles start in corners.

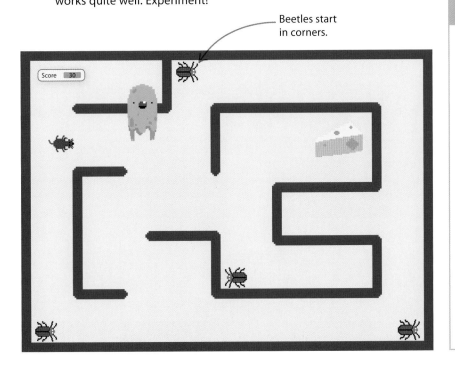

Messages

Messages provide a neat way of making sprites react to each other. We could have made the mouse check whether it's touching a beetle, but that would mean adding "if then" and "touching" blocks to Mimi's code for all four beetles. By using messages, we can add more enemies without changing Mimi's code.

High score

You can make a game more fun by adding a high score for players to beat. We create this in the same way as the score tracker: by making a variable and displaying it on the stage.

45 Select Variables in the blocks palette. Click "Make a Variable" and create a new variable called "High Score". A new block will appear, and the high score counter will appear on the stage. Drag it wherever you like.

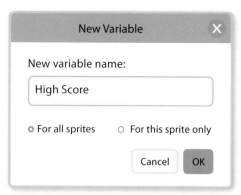

New Variable ✕

New variable name:

High Score

● For all sprites   ○ For this sprite only

Cancel   OK

46 Now add an extra set of blocks to the Cheese sprite's "forever" loop to test for a new high score each time the player gains points. Run the project and see if anyone can beat your high score.

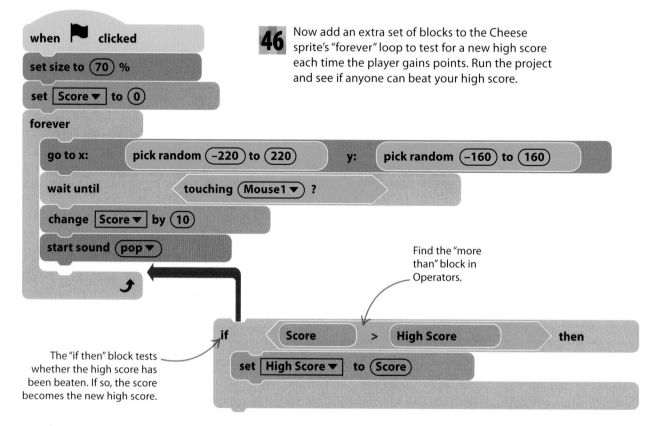

when ⚑ clicked

set size to (70) %

set Score ▼ to (0)

forever

go to x: pick random (-220) to (220)   y: pick random (-160) to (160)

wait until touching (Mouse1 ▼) ?

change Score ▼ by (10)

start sound (pop ▼)

Find the "more than" block in Operators.

if Score > High Score then

set High Score ▼ to (Score)

The "if then" block tests whether the high score has been beaten. If so, the score becomes the new high score.

Game over!

At the moment, the only signal the game has ended is that the mouse stops moving. You can add a finishing touch to any game by displaying a large, bold GAME OVER! sign. To do this, you need to create a sprite and use the "GameOver" message to make it appear.

47 Click the paintbrush symbol 🖌 in the sprites menu to create a new sprite with the paint editor. Using "Bitmap Mode," draw a rectangle and fill it with a dark color. Now switch to "Vector Mode." Choose a bright color and use the text tool to type GAME OVER! in the rectangle. Change the font to "Sans Serif", and use the selection tool to make the text large.

Use the selection tool to enlarge the text.

Change the font to Sans Serif.

48 You don't want the GAME OVER! sign to show until the game is really over, so let's hide it with some code. Switch to the Code tab, and add these blocks.

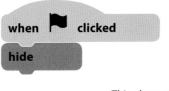

49 Now add some code to make the sprite appear when the game ends. You can use the same message that stops Mimi to trigger this code.

This places the GAME OVER! sign in the middle.

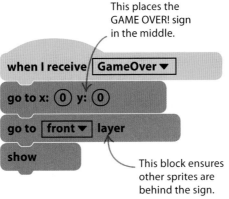

This block ensures other sprites are behind the sign.

50 Run the game. You should now see the GAME OVER! sign when you get caught by a beetle. To make the sign work with the ghost, too, replace its "stop all" block with a "broadcast GameOver" block.

Hacks and tweaks

Take Cheese Chase to the next level by tweaking the rules of the game and the way the sprites behave. You can also experiment with big changes that turn Cheese Chase into a totally different kind of game.

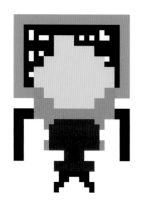

◁ **Play on**
You need to play the game a lot to find out what works and what can be improved. Get other people to play. You can adjust many properties of the game until you get the right configuration: a game where the abilities of the player and enemies are well balanced.

△ **Add sounds**
Jazz up the game with some sound effects using the "start sound" block when the ghost appears, when the game ends, or when you get a high score. There are lots of sounds in Scratch's sound library that you can experiment with.

▷ **Tweak timings**
You might find Cheese Chase harder than Star Hunter. To make it easier, you can make the beetles slower or make the ghost appear for a shorter time. You can also speed up Mimi. For variety, try making each beetle run at a different speed.

▷ **Rocket power**
Add a power boost that hides all the enemies for 10 seconds when the mouse touches it. To do this, you would need to add a new sprite and a message to trigger a hide-wait-show code block in each enemy.

▽ **Vanishing cheese**
For an extra challenge, make the cheese spend only 10 seconds or so in each spot before moving to a new location. This will force the player to move fast. To do this, give the cheese an extra code block with a "forever" loop containing a "wait 10 seconds" block, followed by a copy of the "go to" block from the main code.

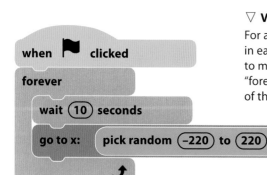

This block picks a random location for the cheese.

▷ Don't touch the walls

Make the game end if Mimi touches the walls of the maze. Add some code to the Maze sprite to send the message "GameOver" if she touches the maze. This makes the game much harder. To make it even harder, try switching the player's controls from the keyboard to the computer mouse. The game then becomes a test of a steady hand.

GAME OVER!

Adding instructions

Players like to see a game's instructions clearly before they start playing. Here are three ways of including instructions.

▽ Project page

The easiest way to include instructions is to simply type them in the instructions box on the project page. You need to log in to an online Scratch account to do this.

▽ Instructions sprite

You can use the paint editor to create an Instructions sprite in the same way that you created the Game Over sprite. Give it the following code to show the sprite at the start of the game and to hide it once the player presses the space bar.

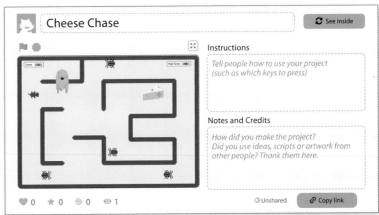

Cheese Chase

Instructions
Tell people how to use your project (such as which keys to press)

Notes and Credits
How did you make the project? Did you use ideas, scripts or artwork from other people? Thank them here.

♡ 0   ★ 0   ⊚ 0   ◉ 1

```
when 🏳 clicked
go to x: 0 y: 0
go to front layer
show
wait until  key space pressed ?
hide
```

The Instructions sprite appears until you press the space bar.

▽ Speech bubbles

Make your game characters tell the player the instructions using speech bubbles. Add a "say" block to the start of Mimi's code to explain the game. Don't forget to add "wait" blocks to the enemies' code—otherwise, there's a risk you'll lose before you start!

```
when 🏳 clicked
set size to 35 %
wait until  key space pressed ?
```

Add this "wait until" block to the start of every other sprite's code so they don't start moving until the game begins.

Do as I say!

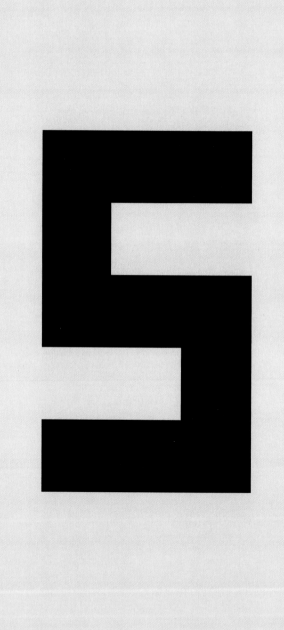

Circle
Wars

How to build Circle Wars

Lightning-fast reactions are essential in Circle Wars, a fast-paced game in which you hunt green circles while being chased by red ones. The game uses Scratch's clones feature, which can turn a single sprite into an army of sinister copies.

AIM OF THE GAME

Move the blue circle around the screen using the mouse. Collect the pale green circles, but avoid the red ones that march toward you like a zombie army. The solid green and solid red circles drop clones of themselves as they roam around. Score more than 20 points to win and go below −20 to lose.

◁ **Player**
The player is the blue circle. If you don't keep moving quickly, the enemy circles will soon overwhelm you.

◁ **Friends**
The friendly circles are green. When you touch one, you score a point, and the circle disappears with a pop.

◁ **Enemies**
Steer clear of the red enemy circles. Touch one and it takes three points off your score, before vanishing with a clash of cymbals.

The timer shows how long each game takes.

The score rises or falls as green and red clones are touched by the player.

Score   8

Time   23.5

The solid green circle lays the friendly clones.

The solid red circle lays the enemy clones.

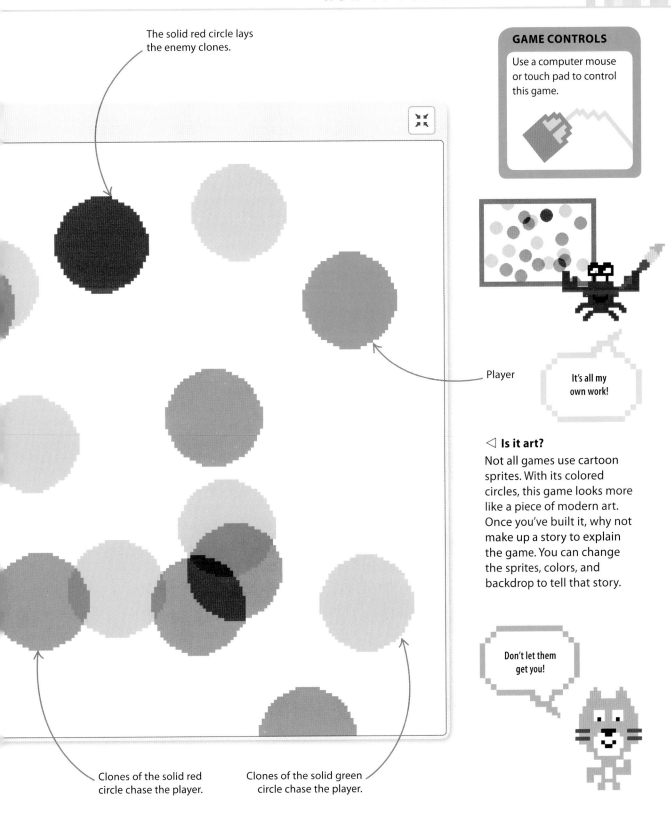

Player

Clones of the solid red circle chase the player.

Clones of the solid green circle chase the player.

GAME CONTROLS

Use a computer mouse or touch pad to control this game.

It's all my own work!

◁ **Is it art?**

Not all games use cartoon sprites. With its colored circles, this game looks more like a piece of modern art. Once you've built it, why not make up a story to explain the game. You can change the sprites, colors, and backdrop to tell that story.

Don't let them get you!

Creating the sprites

First, you need to create the three sprites for the main game. These are all simple colored circles, so you can draw them yourself. Start by following these instructions to create the player's character—the blue circle.

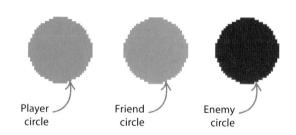

Player _____ circle

Friend _____ circle

Enemy _____ circle

1 Start a new project and name it "Circle Wars". Click the paintbrush symbol in the sprites menu to paint a new sprite.

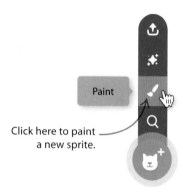

Click here to paint _____ a new sprite.

2 To draw a blue circle, first select "Convert to Bitmap" (bottom left). Then choose blue in the color palette.

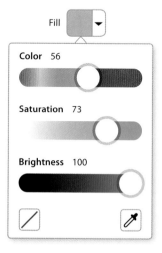

Fill

Color   56

Saturation   73

Brightness   100

3 Click the circle tool on the left, and then select a solid color (instead of an outline) at the top of the paint editor.

Circle tool

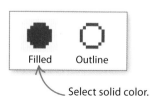

Filled   Outline

Select solid color.

4 While holding down the shift key (this gives you a circle instead of an oval), click with the mouse and drag to draw a circle. The circle should be about the size of the cat's head. When you're happy with the circle's size, delete the cat sprite (right-click on it and select "delete"). Rename the new sprite "Player".

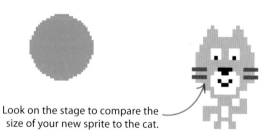

Look on the stage to compare the _____ size of your new sprite to the cat.

∴∴ EXPERT TIPS

Resizing the circle

If your circle is too big or too small, you can change its size by using the "Select" tool. Click and drag the cursor over the sprite in the painting area. A rotation tool will appear.

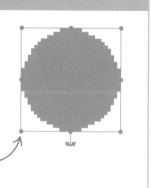

Pull the corner _____ points in or out to change the size.

Making friends and enemies

You can now make the green friend and red enemy circles. You can use other colors if you like, but make sure you can easily tell the three different circles apart.

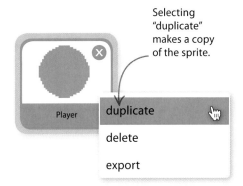

Selecting "duplicate" makes a copy of the sprite.

5 Start by right-clicking on the Player sprite and selecting "duplicate". Do this twice. You'll now have three blue circles. Rename Player2 as "Friends" and Player3 as "Enemies".

6 Select the Friends sprite, and click the Costumes tab. Choose green in the color palette. Select the "Fill" tool, and click inside the blue circle to make it turn green.

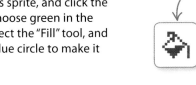

"Fill" tool

Click inside the blue circle to make it green.

I have some friends and quite a few enemies!

7 Repeat the steps for the Enemies sprite, but color this sprite red. You should now have three different-colored sprites.

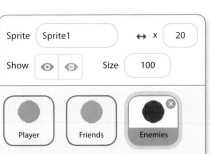

Instant player control

Now add a score display and some code to make the Player sprite stick to the mouse-pointer—just like in Star Hunter.

9 Add the code below to get the blue circle following the mouse. Read it through and make sure you understand what it does. Run the code to make sure it works. The red and green circles won't do anything yet.

8 Select the Player sprite, click Variables, and make a variable called "Score". Then put a check in this variable's box to show "Score" on the stage.

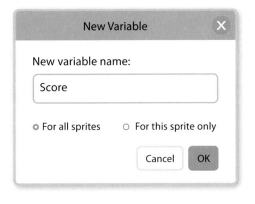

New Variable

New variable name:

Score

⦿ For all sprites ◯ For this sprite only

Cancel OK

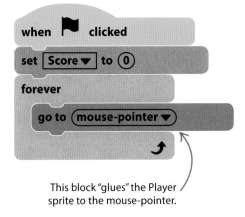

```
when [flag] clicked
set Score ▼ to (0)
forever
    go to (mouse-pointer ▼)
```

This block "glues" the Player sprite to the mouse-pointer.

March of the clones

From just two sprites—the green and red circles—you can create an army of friends and enemies to pursue the player's blue circle. You can do this through the magic of cloning. Before you create your clones, first get the Friends sprite moving randomly around the stage.

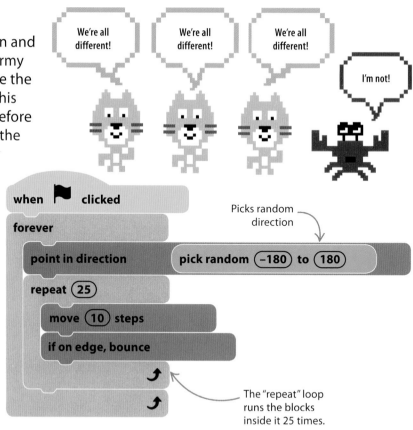

10 Select the green Friends sprite. Add this code to make the circle bounce around the stage with a random change of direction every 250 steps.

Picks random direction

```
when 🏳 clicked
forever
    point in direction    pick random (-180) to (180)
    repeat (25)
        move (10) steps
        if on edge, bounce
```

The "repeat" loop runs the blocks inside it 25 times.

11 Run the project, and watch the green circle's unpredictable journey. The Friends sprite moves 250 steps in 10-step jumps, but it doesn't get stuck to the walls. After 250 steps, the "forever" loop goes back to the start. The sprite changes direction randomly and sets off again.

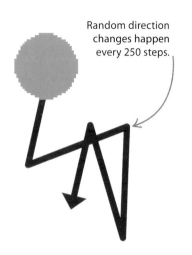

Random direction changes happen every 250 steps.

Repeat loops

You've already seen "forever" loops that repeat a group of blocks nonstop. A "repeat" loop does a similar job, but it repeats the blocks inside only a fixed number of times. This type of loop is sometimes called a "for" loop, because it repeats *for* a certain number of times. The example shown here repeats an action four times to draw a square.

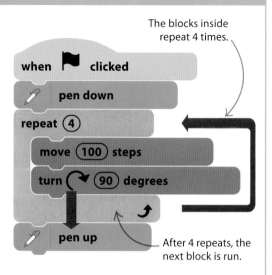

The blocks inside repeat 4 times.

```
when 🏳 clicked
    pen down
repeat (4)
    move (100) steps
    turn ↻ (90) degrees
    pen up
```

After 4 repeats, the next block is run.

Making clones

Now we're going to make our friendly clone army. These are the clones you need to catch to score points.

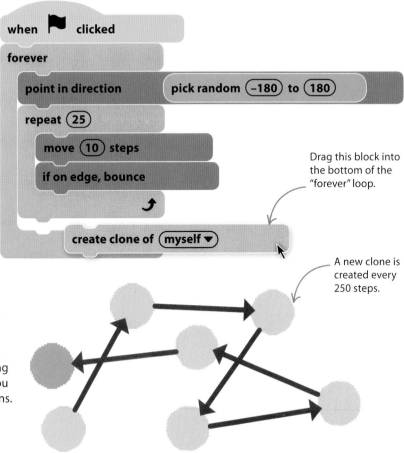

12 Add a "create clone of myself" block as the last block in the "forever" loop. You'll find it in the orange Control section. This block will create a clone of the Friends sprite after each 250-step movement.

Drag this block into the bottom of the "forever" loop.

A new clone is created every 250 steps.

13 Run the project. At each change of direction, the sprite leaves a copy of itself—a clone. The clones aren't just pictures—they are fully working copies of the original sprite, and you can give them their own instructions.

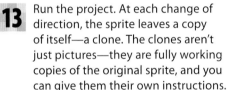

14 New clones are controlled by the "when I start as a clone" block. Add the code below to the Friends sprite. The code tells each clone to move toward the Player sprite for 300 steps, after which the clone is deleted and vanishes from the stage. The clones move one step at a time. They move more slowly than the original Friends sprite, which moves in 10-step jumps.

All clones run their own copy of this code.

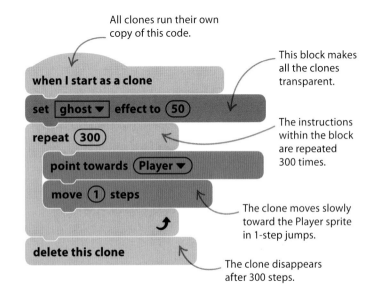

This block makes all the clones transparent.

The instructions within the block are repeated 300 times.

The clone moves slowly toward the Player sprite in 1-step jumps.

15 Run the code and watch the green clones advance slowly toward the Player sprite. Don't worry—they're the good guys!

The clone disappears after 300 steps.

Destroying clones

The last part of the code for the Friends clone checks if the clone is touching the Player. If it is, the clone gets deleted.

16 Add an "if then" block containing the blocks shown here to check whether the clone is touching the Player sprite after each move. Try running the project now—the score should increase as you touch green circles, which instantly disappear with a pop.

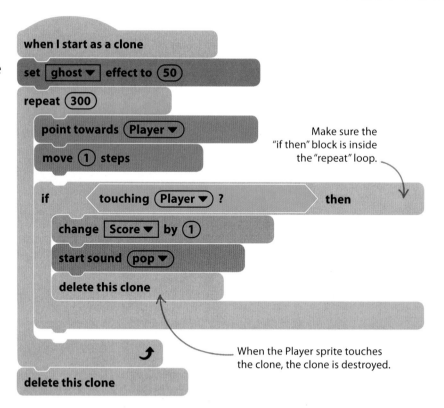

```
when I start as a clone
set ghost ▼ effect to 50
repeat 300
    point towards Player ▼
    move 1 steps
    if  touching Player ▼ ?  then
        change Score ▼ by 1
        start sound pop ▼
        delete this clone
delete this clone
```

Make sure the "if then" block is inside the "repeat" loop.

When the Player sprite touches the clone, the clone is destroyed.

POP!

EXPERT TIPS

Clones

Clones are useful any time you want lots of copies of a sprite. Many programming languages let you make copies of things, but they are often called objects instead of clones.

Such languages are called "object-oriented" languages and include Java and C++. In Scratch, there are three orange blocks that control clones, all found in the Control section.

create clone of myself ▼

△ This block creates a clone of the sprite. The clone is identical to the sprite and appears in the same position and facing the same direction, so you won't be able to see it until it moves.

delete this clone

△ This block gets rid of the clone. All clones disappear from the stage when a project stops, leaving just the original sprite.

when I start as a clone

△ When a clone starts, it runs the code headed with this block. Clones don't run the sprite's main code, but they can run all other code blocks in the sprite's code area, such as code blocks triggered by messages.

Enemy clones

Now you need to add code blocks to the Enemies sprite to make it produce clones that chase the Player. You can do this by copying the code from the Friends sprite across to the Enemies sprite.

17 To copy code blocks, just click, drag, and drop code blocks from one sprite onto another. Drag the two code blocks you made for the Friends sprite onto the Enemies sprite, one at a time. This makes copies of the code in the Enemies sprite.

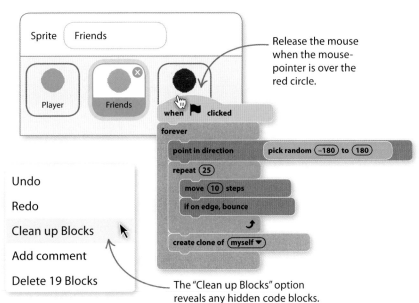

Release the mouse when the mouse-pointer is over the red circle.

Sprite | Friends

Player | Friends

when 🏴 clicked
forever
  point in direction | pick random (−180) to (180)
  repeat (25)
    move (10) steps
    if on edge, bounce
  create clone of (myself ▼)

18 Select the Enemies sprite. The code blocks you dragged and dropped may be on top of one another. To rearrange them, right-click on the background and select "Clean up Blocks".

Undo
Redo
Clean up Blocks
Add comment
Delete 19 Blocks

The "Clean up Blocks" option reveals any hidden code blocks.

19 Now adjust the Enemies clone code so that it takes points away when the Player touches a red clone. Alter the "change Score by" block so it changes the score by −3 instead of +1. You really want to avoid those nasty red enemies!

change | Score ▼ | by (−3)

This reduces the player's score by 3 points.

Change the code to play a cymbal sound.

20 Add a sound to tell the player that points have been lost. Load the cymbal sound into the Enemies sprite by selecting "Cymbal" in the sound library. Alter the code to play "Cymbal", not "pop". You'll now hear which type of clone you've touched.

start sound (Cymbal ▼)

She may not be the best player, but she is the loudest!

21 Run the project. Check that you now have both red and green clones and that touching a red clone takes 3 points off your score.

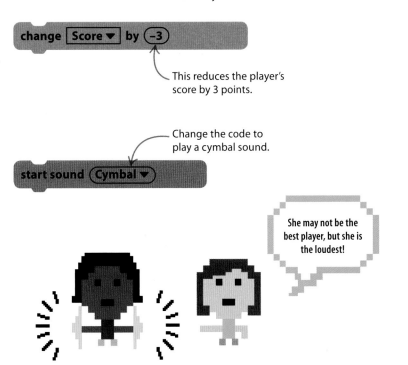

Win or lose?

You've created two ever-expanding clone armies: one of friendly circles that help you win points, and one of evil circles that make you lose points. Next, you need to add the code that tells you whether you've won or lost the game.

22 Add the new "if then" blocks shown here to the Player sprite. They check your score. If the score is greater than 20, you win, and a thought bubble with the word "Victory!" appears. If the score is less than –20, you lose, and the sprite thinks "Defeat!"

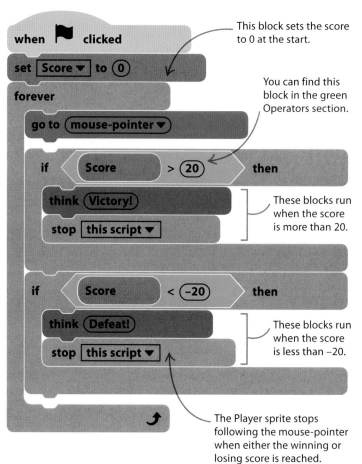

This block sets the score to 0 at the start.

You can find this block in the green Operators section.

These blocks run when the score is more than 20.

These blocks run when the score is less than –20.

The Player sprite stops following the mouse-pointer when either the winning or losing score is reached.

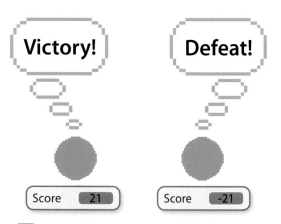

Comparison operators

Earlier we saw how you can use "if then" blocks to create true or false statements—also known as Boolean expressions—that lead to different outcomes. For example, in Star Hunter, "if touching cat then play sound Fairydust" makes a sound play only when the cat gets a star. We can do the same thing with numbers by using what are called comparison operators:

is less than   equals   is more than

When we add these to "if then" blocks, they create statements that are either true or false. In Circle Wars, the "is more than" operator tells you that you've won the game when you score over 20.

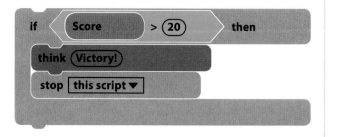

23 Run the game. Try to touch only the green circles. Make sure the game ends when the key scores are reached, and make sure the Player sprite thinks "Victory!" or "Defeat!" You can reduce the score needed to win if you find it too difficult. But don't make the game too easy—Circle Wars is meant to be a challenge!

I am the champion!

Adding a timer

To add some competition to the game, you can include an on-screen timer that shows players how long they take to complete a game.

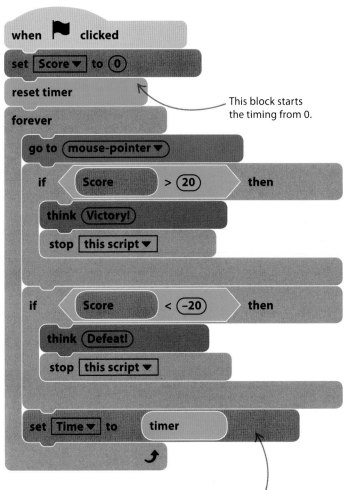

This block starts the timing from 0.

 24 Click on the Variables section, and make a variable "Time" for all sprites. To show it on the stage, check the box next to the variable's block. Select the Player sprite. Click on Sensing in the blocks palette. Add "reset timer" to the Player's code, just before the "forever" loop. Go back to Variables, and drag a "set Time to" block to the code and add "timer" to it, making it the last instruction in the forever loop.

25 By copying "timer" to the variable "Time", each trip around the loop will now display the time on the stage. But the moment the player wins or loses, the time stops being updated (the code is stopped), and the total time it took to win or lose is shown.

Time 41.573

Total number of seconds in the game

I think it must be lunchtime!

This block updates the Time display every time the loop repeats.

Instructions

Players need to know the rules of the game. Create a special sprite that shows the instructions for Circle Wars when the game begins.

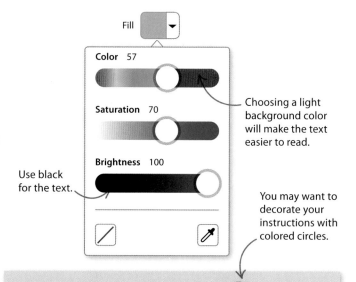

Fill

Color 57

Saturation 70

Brightness 100

Choosing a light background color will make the text easier to read.

Use black for the text.

You may want to decorate your instructions with colored circles.

26 Use the paintbrush symbol to create a new sprite and rename it "Instructions". Select "Convert to Bitmap" and choose a color. Select the "Fill" tool, and click on the drawing area to fill it with your chosen color.

"Fill" tool

27 Now select black from the palette as the color for the text. Then choose the text tool and type out the instructions shown here.

"Text" tool

28 If the text doesn't fit, use the select tool to resize it by pulling the corner points in or out. When you've finished, click outside the box around the text to stop editing.

"Select" tool

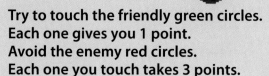

You are the blue circle.
Move using the mouse.
Be quick!

Try to touch the friendly green circles.
Each one gives you 1 point.
Avoid the enemy red circles.
Each one you touch takes 3 points.

Score more than 20 to win.
Score less than –20 and you lose.

Press the space bar to start!

GAME DESIGN

Game stories

Computer games usually have a story to explain why the action in the game is happening. At the moment, Circle Wars has no story. Can you make one up? It could be a battle in space, with a blue spaceship saving friendly green spaceships and trying to avoid being hit by the red enemy craft. Let your imagination run wild! Including some of the story in your instructions will help make the game more interesting and exciting for the player.

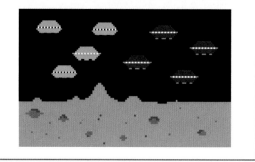

29 Add this code to the sprite to show the instructions on the stage at the start of the game. Read it carefully. Can you see how it works?

These blocks show the instructions in the center of the screen in front of other sprites.

This block hides the Instruction sprite when the player presses the space bar to start playing.

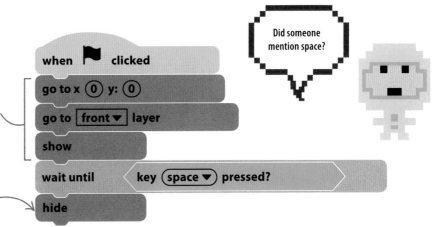

Did someone mention space?

```
when ⚑ clicked
go to x (0) y: (0)
go to [front ▼] layer
show
wait until  key (space ▼) pressed?
hide
```

30 You also need to add a "wait until key space pressed" block immediately after the green flag blocks in the Player, Friends, and Enemies sprites' code. This will hold back all the action until the space bar is pressed.

Add a "wait until key space pressed" block to the code of all three sprites.

31 Run the project, and your instructions should appear, filling the screen until you press the space bar. Players will have plenty of time to read and understand the instructions, letting them start the game when they're ready.

I'm ready to play!

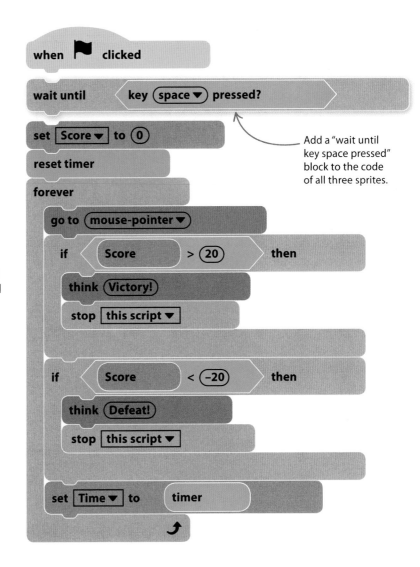

```
when ⚑ clicked
wait until  key (space ▼) pressed?
set [Score ▼] to (0)
reset timer
forever
    go to (mouse-pointer ▼)
    if < Score > (20) > then
        think (Victory!)
        stop [this script ▼]
    if < Score < (-20) > then
        think (Defeat!)
        stop [this script ▼]
    set [Time ▼] to  timer
```

Hacks and tweaks

You've got Circle Wars working—well done! Now to personalize it and make it your own. Try these suggestions and your own ideas. Once you've created something unique, why not share it on the Scratch projects website?

△ **Find a balance**
Experiment with different speeds, or change how many points you win or lose for touching Friends and Enemies. It's not difficult to make the game very hard or very easy, but can you find a balance to make it just the right level?

▽ **What's the story?**
Did you think of a story to explain what's going on in Circle Wars? Maybe it's the attack of the dragons, and the princess player has to eat cakes to survive? Add some scenery and music to the game to fit with that story. Experiment with different stories and looks.

▷ **The war's over!**
Add a broadcast message to reveal a Game Over sprite when the player wins or loses, like you did in Cheese Chase. You can change the text of the Game Over sprite so that it relates to your story about the game.

▷ **Slow down, blue!**
To make things tricky, change the blue circle's code so that it no longer "sticks" to the mouse-pointer but chases slowly after it. You could also invent simple keyboard controls for the sprite.

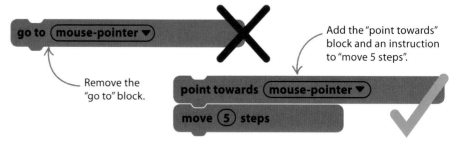

Remove the "go to" block.

Add the "point towards" block and an instruction to "move 5 steps".

▽ **Tweak the timer**
The number in the timer flickers because it shows lots of decimal places. To round the value so it shows only whole seconds, use the green "round" block near the bottom of the Operators section. Try adding a "Best time" for winning players, just as you added a "High score" in Cheese Chase.

That's their best time yet!

▽ **Change the colors**

Vary the clones' colors. Click on the Friends sprite. Add the "set color effect to" block from the Looks section to the sprite's clone code. Then drag "pick random" from Operators into the block's window and change the values to −30 and 30. Do the same for the Enemies sprite. New clones will now have different colors!

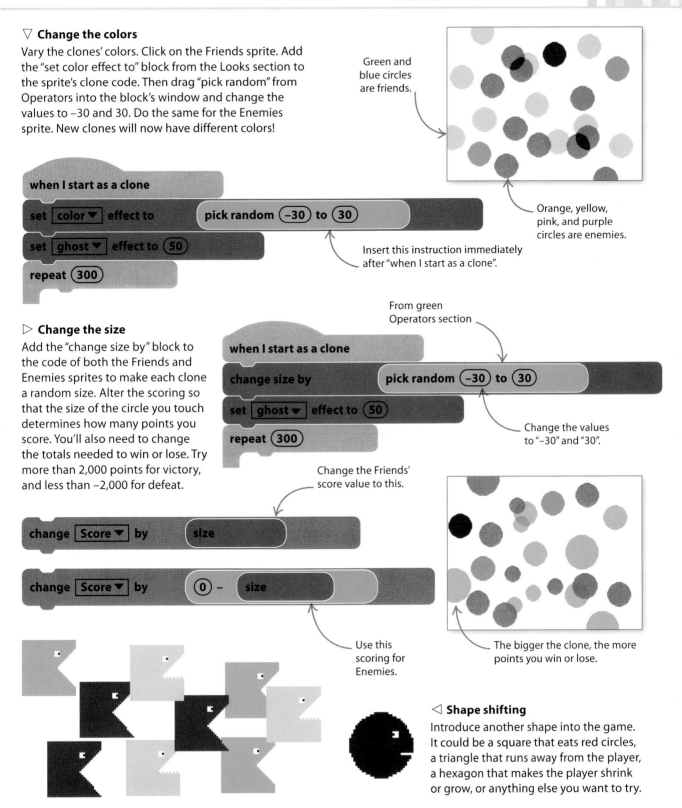

Green and blue circles are friends.

Orange, yellow, pink, and purple circles are enemies.

```
when I start as a clone
set  color ▼  effect to        pick random  (−30)  to  (30)
set  ghost ▼  effect to  (50)
repeat  (300)
```

Insert this instruction immediately after "when I start as a clone".

▷ **Change the size**

Add the "change size by" block to the code of both the Friends and Enemies sprites to make each clone a random size. Alter the scoring so that the size of the circle you touch determines how many points you score. You'll also need to change the totals needed to win or lose. Try more than 2,000 points for victory, and less than −2,000 for defeat.

From green Operators section

```
when I start as a clone
change size by        pick random  (−30)  to  (30)
set  ghost ▼  effect to  (50)
repeat  (300)
```

Change the values to "−30" and "30".

Change the Friends' score value to this.

```
change  Score ▼  by        size
```

```
change  Score ▼  by      (0) −   size
```

Use this scoring for Enemies.

The bigger the clone, the more points you win or lose.

◁ **Shape shifting**

Introduce another shape into the game. It could be a square that eats red circles, a triangle that runs away from the player, a hexagon that makes the player shrink or grow, or anything else you want to try.

Jumpy Monkey

How to build Jumpy Monkey

In the real world, there are laws you just can't break. For example, the law of gravity means that something that goes up must always come down again. Jumpy Monkey shows you how to add gravity to your game worlds.

AIM OF THE GAME

The monkey is on a mission to collect bananas. Choose which direction he leaps in and how fast he goes. You need to send him over the palm tree to grab the bananas using the fewest possible jumps.

◁ **Launcher**
Point this arrow in the direction you want to launch the monkey by using the left and right arrow keys.

◁ **Monkey**
Select the monkey's launch speed with the up and down arrow keys, and then press the space bar to launch him.

◁ **Bananas**
If the monkey touches any of the bananas, he will eat them. Keep going until he eats all the bananas.

The instructions appear on the game at the start.

SET LAUNCH ANGLE ← →
SET LAUNCH SPEED ↑ ↓
PRESS SPACE TO FIRE

The monkey is launched from the arrow when you press the space bar.

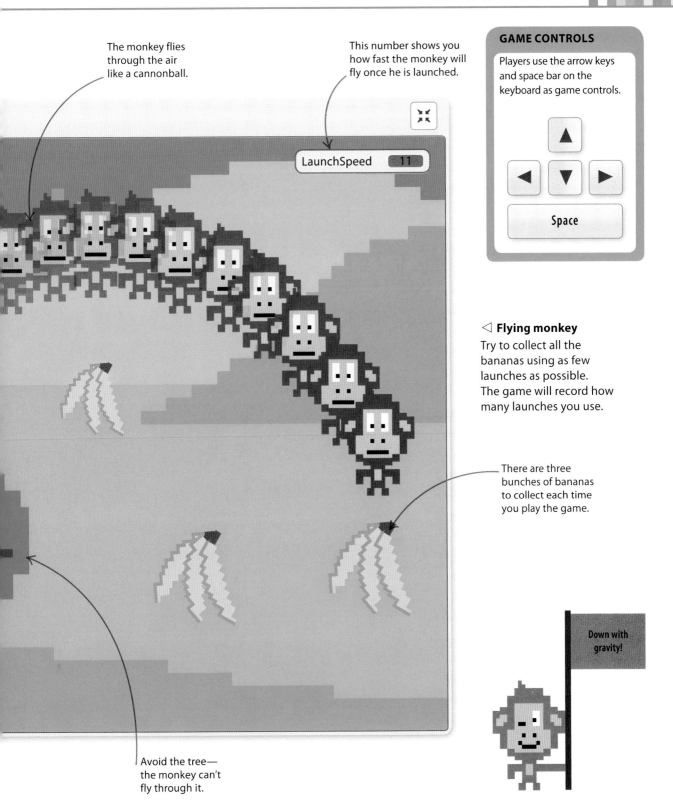

The monkey flies through the air like a cannonball.

This number shows you how fast the monkey will fly once he is launched.

LaunchSpeed 11

GAME CONTROLS

Players use the arrow keys and space bar on the keyboard as game controls.

▲

◀ ▼ ▶

Space

◁ **Flying monkey**
Try to collect all the bananas using as few launches as possible. The game will record how many launches you use.

There are three bunches of bananas to collect each time you play the game.

Avoid the tree—the monkey can't fly through it.

Down with gravity!

Launching the monkey

This game uses a big arrow to help the player choose the monkey's precise launch direction. We'll ignore gravity to start off with, but you'll need to add it later to get the monkey past the tree.

1 Start a new project and call it "Jumpy Monkey." Delete the cat sprite and load two sprites from the library—"Monkey" and "Arrow1". Select the arrow sprite and rename it "Launcher".

2 Go to Variables, select "Make a Variable", and add a variable called "LaunchSpeed". The new variable will automatically show up on the stage. Drag it to the top right of the window.

Type here to rename the sprite.

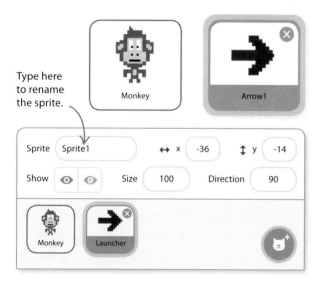

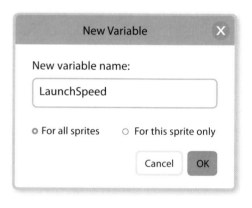

3 Select the Launcher sprite, and then add these three code blocks to set up the Launcher and allow the player to control its angle using the left and right arrow keys on the keyboard. The direction of the arrow is the direction that the monkey will launch in. Run the code and try turning the arrow.

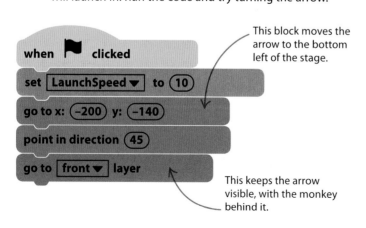

This block moves the arrow to the bottom left of the stage.

This keeps the arrow visible, with the monkey behind it.

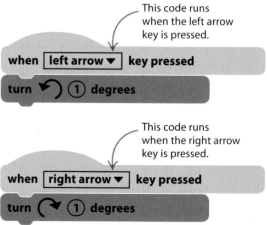

This code runs when the left arrow key is pressed.

This code runs when the right arrow key is pressed.

4 Now that you can aim, you need controls to set the speed of the launch. Add these code blocks to change the speed using the up and down arrow keys.

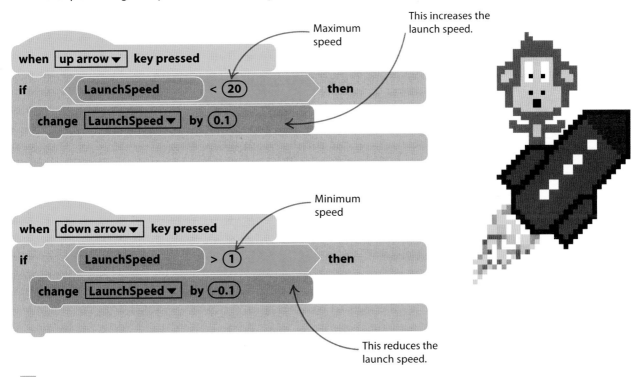

Maximum speed

This increases the launch speed.

```
when up arrow ▼ key pressed
if       LaunchSpeed    < 20    then
    change LaunchSpeed ▼ by 0.1
```

Minimum speed

```
when down arrow ▼ key pressed
if       LaunchSpeed    > 1    then
    change LaunchSpeed ▼ by -0.1
```

This reduces the launch speed.

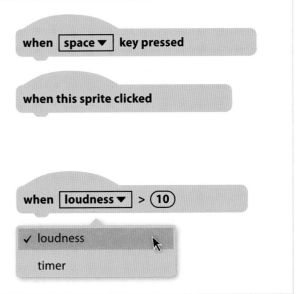

LINGO

Events

The key presses and mouse clicks that a computer detects are known as events. The yellow Events blocks in Scratch trigger blocks of code whenever a particular event occurs. We've seen them used with messages in Cheese Chase, but Scratch also lets you trigger code blocks using keys, mouse clicks, sound levels, and even movement detected by a webcam. Don't be afraid to experiment.

```
when space ▼ key pressed
```

```
when this sprite clicked
```

```
when loudness ▼ > 10
```

```
✓ loudness
  timer
```

▷ **Setting things off**
Events blocks such as these are used to trigger a code whenever the event they describe occurs.

5 Now select the Monkey sprite. Add this code to shrink him down to the right size and move him behind the Launcher.

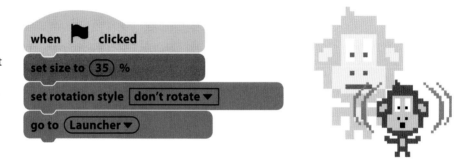

when ⚑ clicked
set size to (35) %
set rotation style [don't rotate ▼]
go to (Launcher ▼)

6 To launch the monkey when the space bar is pressed, add this new code to the Monkey sprite. "Repeat until" is a new type of loop block that keeps repeating the block inside until the condition becomes true—in this case, the monkey keeps moving until it touches the edge of the stage.

This makes the monkey's direction match the direction of the launch arrow.

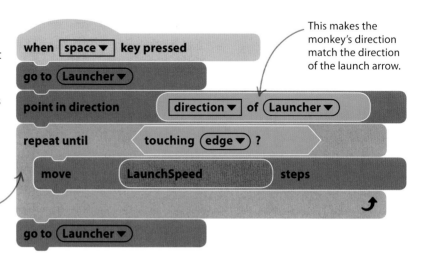

when [space ▼] key pressed
go to (Launcher ▼)
point in direction [direction ▼] of (Launcher ▼)
repeat until < touching (edge ▼) ? >
    move (LaunchSpeed) steps
go to (Launcher ▼)

The "repeat until" block keeps the monkey moving to the edge of the stage.

"repeat until"

Do you want to keep repeating an action only until something happens and then move on to the rest of the code? The "repeat until" block can help your code when "forever" and "repeat" loops aren't flexible enough. Most programming languages use similar loops, but some call them "while" loops—these continue *while* the condition is true instead of looping *until* the condition is true. There are always different ways to think about the same problem.

7 Try setting the Launcher angle and speed using the arrow keys, and pressing the space bar to fire the monkey. He goes in a completely straight line until he hits the edge of the stage. Real things don't do this—they fall back toward the ground as they move. We'll add gravity to the game later to make the monkey behave realistically.

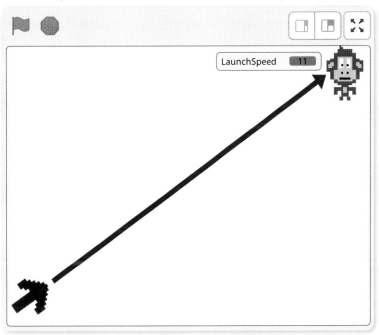

LaunchSpeed 11

Bananas and trees

The point of this game is for the monkey to collect bananas. By using clones, you can add just one Bananas sprite but give the monkey plenty of fruit to aim for.

8 Add the Bananas sprite to the project. Make a variable for all sprites called "NumBananas" to keep track of the number of bananas on the stage—start with three. Make sure to uncheck its check box. Build the following code to clone the bananas, but don't run it yet because you still need to tell the clones what to do.

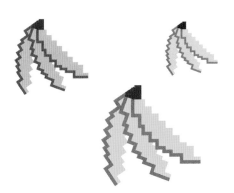

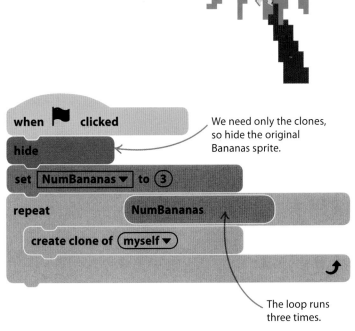

when 🏳 clicked

hide

set NumBananas ▼ to ③

repeat   NumBananas

    create clone of myself ▼

We need only the clones, so hide the original Bananas sprite.

The loop runs three times.

9 Add the next bit of code to place each banana clone in a random spot on the right of the stage, change how it looks, and make sure it's not hidden. The clone will wait for the monkey to touch it and then disappear. If it's the last banana, it sends a "GameOver" message, which you need to create as a new message.

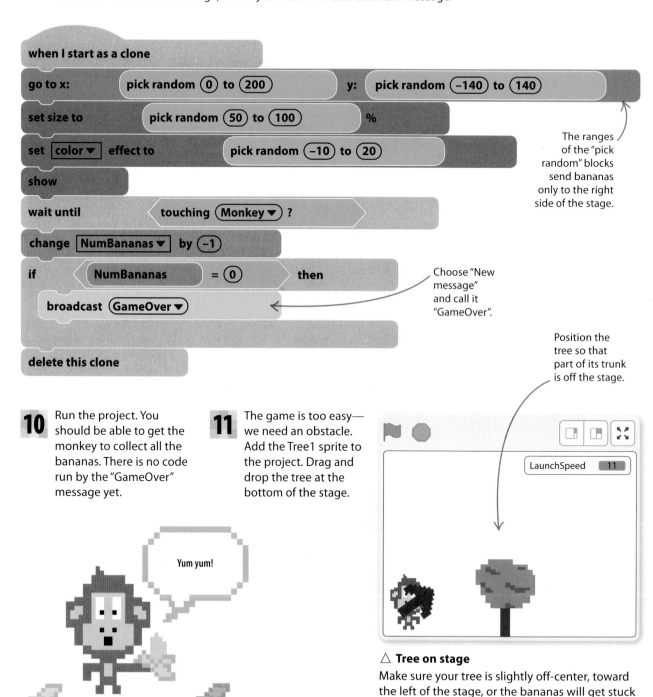

```
when I start as a clone
go to x:   pick random (0) to (200)        y:   pick random (–140) to (140)
set size to        pick random (50) to (100)        %
set   color ▼   effect to        pick random (–10) to (20)
show
wait until        touching (Monkey ▼) ?
change  NumBananas ▼  by (–1)
if        NumBananas        = (0)        then
    broadcast (GameOver ▼)

delete this clone
```

The ranges of the "pick random" blocks send bananas only to the right side of the stage.

Choose "New message" and call it "GameOver".

Position the tree so that part of its trunk is off the stage.

10 Run the project. You should be able to get the monkey to collect all the bananas. There is no code run by the "GameOver" message yet.

11 The game is too easy— we need an obstacle. Add the Tree1 sprite to the project. Drag and drop the tree at the bottom of the stage.

Yum yum!

LaunchSpeed   11

△ **Tree on stage**
Make sure your tree is slightly off-center, toward the left of the stage, or the bananas will get stuck behind the tree and the game won't work.

12 At the moment, the monkey can fly straight through the tree. Change his code so that he stops flying if he touches it.

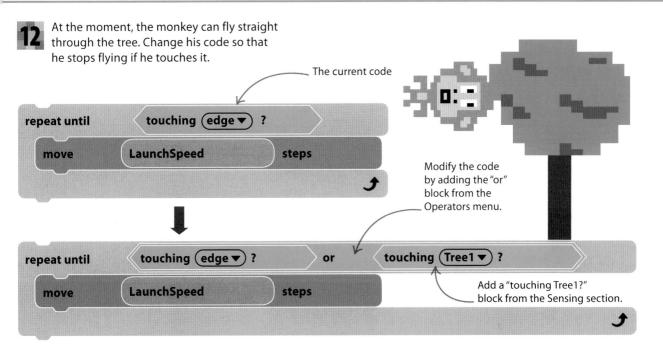

The current code

```
repeat until                touching ( edge ▼ ) ?
    move              LaunchSpeed            steps
```

Modify the code by adding the "or" block from the Operators menu.

```
repeat until       touching ( edge ▼ ) ?       or       touching ( Tree1 ▼ ) ?
    move              LaunchSpeed            steps
```

Add a "touching Tree1?" block from the Sensing section.

13 Run the project. The monkey should stop flying when he hits the tree, which makes any bananas to the right of the tree impossible to reach. Don't worry, gravity will come to the rescue soon.

I want those bananas!

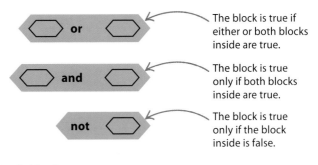

14 Make two more variables for all sprites: "FallSpeed" and "Gravity". Then add a "set Gravity" block to the monkey's "when clicked" code, and amend his "when space key pressed" code as shown below. The new blocks use variables to simulate gravity. "FallSpeed" keeps track of how many steps the monkey needs to be moved down by gravity. The value of "Gravity" is how much "FallSpeed" increases each time the monkey moves.

Variables

[Make a Variable]

☐ **FallSpeed**

☐ **Gravity**

☑ **LaunchSpeed**

☐ **my variable**

☐ **NumBananas**

Uncheck the box next to a variable to make it not appear on the stage.

△ **Hiding variables**

If you don't want variables to appear on the stage, you need to uncheck the box next to them in the Variables section. Do this for these two new variables.

```
when 🚩 clicked
set size to (35) %
set rotation style  don't rotate ▼
go to (Launcher ▼)
set  Gravity ▼  to (-0.2)
```

Add this block to the "when clicked" code.

This new block shows that at the moment of launch, the monkey isn't falling yet.

```
when  space ▼  key pressed
go to (Launcher ▼)
point in direction ( direction ▼ of (Launcher ▼) )
set  FallSpeed ▼  to (0)
repeat until < touching (edge ▼) ? > or < touching (Tree1 ▼) ? >
    move ( LaunchSpeed ) steps
    change y by ( FallSpeed )
    change  FallSpeed ▼  by ( Gravity )
go to (Launcher ▼)
```

This new block moves the monkey down.

This new block contains the variable "Gravity", which makes the monkey fall faster each time the loop runs.

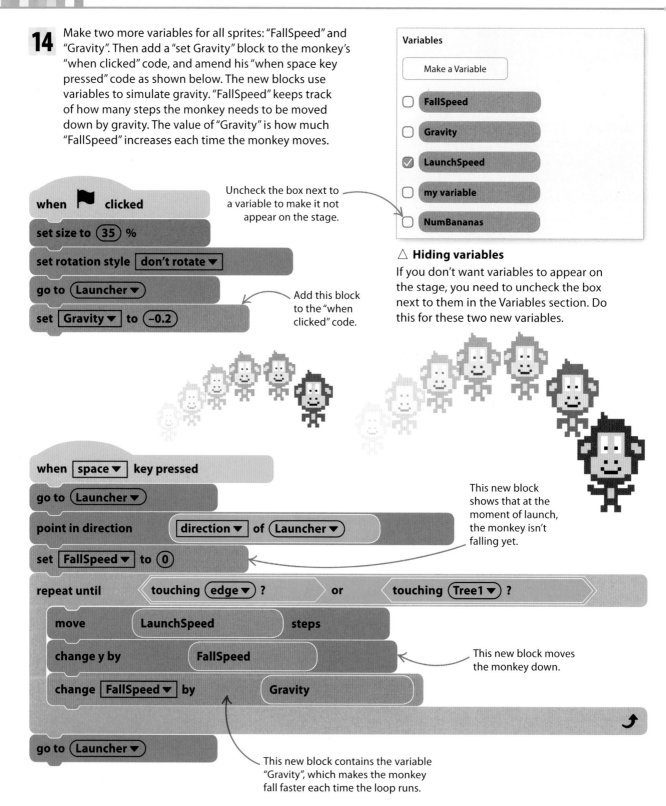

Real-world gravity

In the real world, when you try to throw something in a straight line, it curves slowly back toward the ground as gravity pulls it down. To make the game work in the same way, you move the monkey along the straight line but also add a downward move after each shift along that line, to create the same effect as the constant downward tug of gravity. This allows the monkey's movement to seem natural, making the game more engaging.

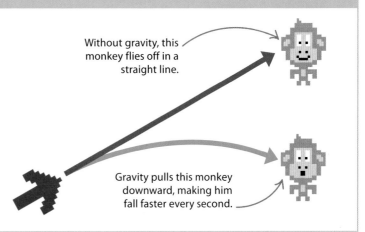

Without gravity, this monkey flies off in a straight line.

Gravity pulls this monkey downward, making him fall faster every second.

15 Run the project again—you can now direct the monkey over the tree to reach the tricky low bananas. But how exactly is the Scratch gravity working? Every second, the monkey falls a little bit faster than the second before, creating a downward curve.

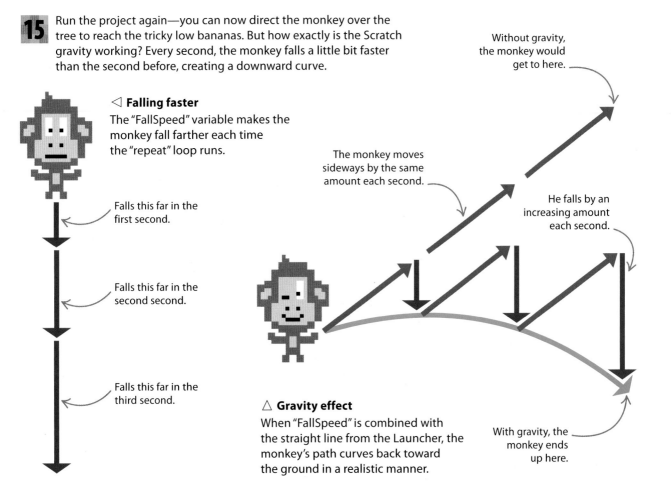

Without gravity, the monkey would get to here.

◁ **Falling faster**
The "FallSpeed" variable makes the monkey fall farther each time the "repeat" loop runs.

The monkey moves sideways by the same amount each second.

He falls by an increasing amount each second.

Falls this far in the first second.

Falls this far in the second second.

Falls this far in the third second.

△ **Gravity effect**
When "FallSpeed" is combined with the straight line from the Launcher, the monkey's path curves back toward the ground in a realistic manner.

With gravity, the monkey ends up here.

Game over

When the monkey has collected all the bananas, a "GameOver" message is broadcast, ending the game. Make a sign to go with it to tell the player how many launches were used to collect the bananas.

16 Click the paintbrush symbol ✏ to paint a new sprite and make a sign like the one below, leaving a gap in the text where the number of launches will go. You can make the sign as plain or as decorative as you like. Name the new sprite "GameOver".

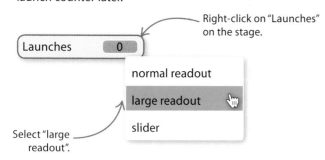

Leave a gap here.

18 Now add these code blocks to your sign. Together, they will count the number of times you launch the monkey and will display that number at the end of the game.

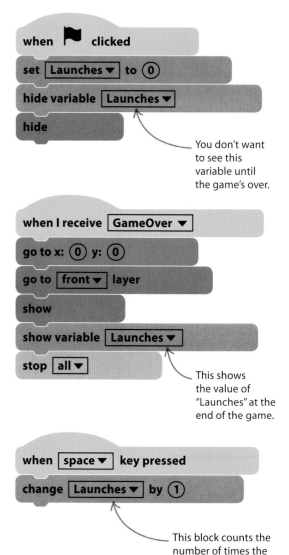

You don't want to see this variable until the game's over.

This shows the value of "Launches" at the end of the game.

This block counts the number of times the space bar is pressed.

17 Now add a variable for all sprites to count the number of launches. Call this variable "Launches", show it on the stage, and right-click on it to change it to "large readout". This shows just the value and not the name of the variable. You'll reposition the launch counter later.

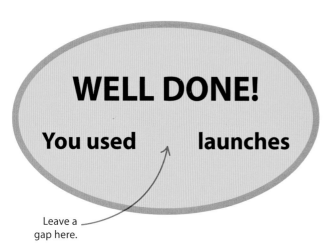

Right-click on "Launches" on the stage.

Select "large readout".

19 Run the game, and collect all the bananas. When you see the WELL DONE! sign on the stage, drag the "Launches" counter into the gap in the sign. Scratch will remember its position in future games, so the sign will always be in the right place.

Drag the "Launches" number into the gap you left in the sign.

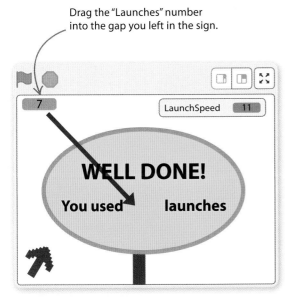

20 To add a backdrop, click on the stage information area in the bottom right, and then choose the Backdrop tab at the top. Either paint your own scenery or load an image from the library. Use the text tool to add the game's instructions to the image, as shown below.

Draw the arrows with the pencil or paintbrush tool.

Make some noise

To make the game more interesting, you can add some sound effects. Follow the instructions below to play different sounds when the monkey is launched and when he eats the bananas.

21 Click the Monkey sprite, select the Sounds tab, and load "Boing" from the library. Then add a "start sound" block to the existing monkey code in the position shown here. This will make the "boing" sound play every time the monkey jumps.

Add this sound block to the existing Monkey code.

22 Click the Bananas sprite, and load "Chomp" from the sound library. Then add a "start sound" block to the existing banana code in the position shown here. Now the "chomping" sound will play each time the monkey gets a banana.

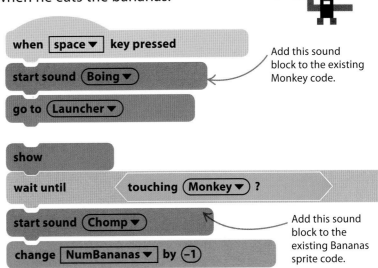

Add this sound block to the existing Bananas sprite code.

Playing with gravity

Add a slider to the game to allow you to experiment with the "Gravity" variable. The slider will allow you to tweak the "Gravity" value—you can even make the monkey fall upward.

23 To adjust gravity in your game world, show the "Gravity" variable on the stage by checking its box in the Variables section. Then right-click the variable display on the stage and select "slider". The slider lets you change the value of a variable on the stage.

Gravity -0.2

normal readout
large readout
slider

Select the "slider" option.

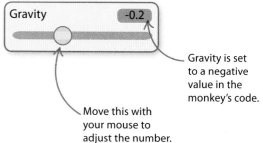

Gravity -0.2

Gravity is set to a negative value in the monkey's code.

Move this with your mouse to adjust the number.

EXPERT TIPS

Displaying variables

You can change how a variable is shown on the stage. There are three different options: normal readout, large readout, and slider. You can also hide the variable using this menu. Choose the look that works best for your game.

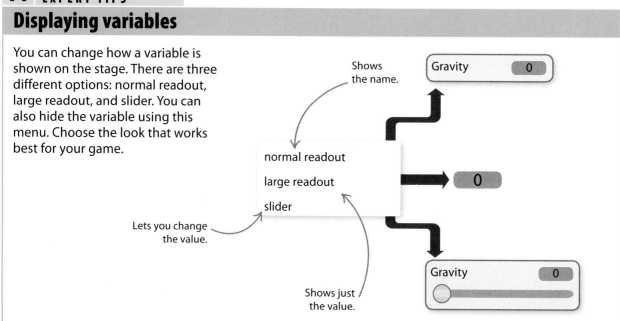

Shows the name.

Gravity 0

normal readout
large readout
slider

Lets you change the value.

0

Shows just the value.

Gravity 0

24 Now play around with the gravity settings in this game using the slider. Using the suggested value of –0.2 in the code works well, but take a look at what happens when you increase or decrease this number using the slider—if it is positive, the monkey will fall upward.

25 When you've finished experimenting with gravity, right-click on the slider and select "hide" to return the game to normal. Now that you know how gravity works, you could try making a version of the game with reverse gravity so the monkey falls upward. Think about what changes you'd need to make to the game for this to work, like moving the Launcher to fire downward.

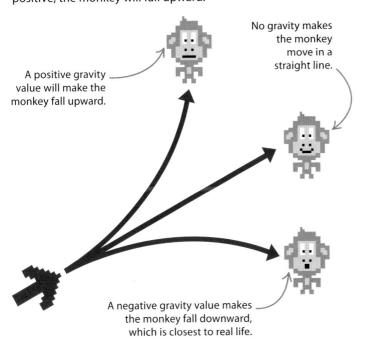

No gravity makes the monkey move in a straight line.

A positive gravity value will make the monkey fall upward.

A negative gravity value makes the monkey fall downward, which is closest to real life.

Help!!!

Game physics

Physics is the science of forces and movement in the real world. Game physics is all about getting that science into games so that things react and move around in realistic ways—being pulled down by gravity, for instance, or bouncing. Programmers have to solve all types of physics problems to make games more realistic or fun. When objects collide, should they bounce or crunch? How should objects move when they go underwater or into space?

△ **Defying gravity**
Game physics doesn't have to be like real-world physics—you can create worlds with gravity that makes things fall upward or even sideways. Gravity can be much stronger or weaker than in real life—perhaps balls fly higher with each bounce, until they shoot off into space.

Hacks and tweaks

Congratulations—you've built your first game with gravity. Once you've tried the game a few times, you can start to play around with the code to make the game your own. Here are a few ideas to try out.

◁ **Banana bonanza**
Try adding more bananas, making them bigger or smaller, and putting them in different places on the screen.

▽ **Fruit salad**
Add more fruits with a different score for each type. You'll need to make a "Score" variable and add extra sprites—there are oranges and watermelons in the Scratch sprite library.

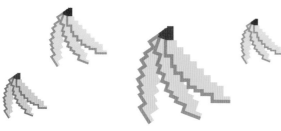

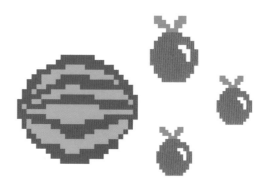

▽ **Beat the clock**
You can add a timer to make the player complete the game in a set time. Create a new variable called "TimeLeft", and add the code below to the Monkey sprite. Then create a new sprite, click on the Costumes tab, and make a sign that says "Time's Up". Finally, add the two code blocks on the right to this sprite.

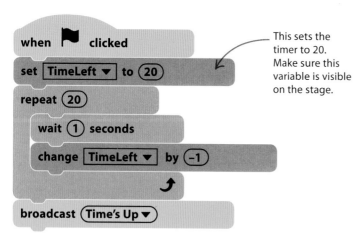

This sets the timer to 20. Make sure this variable is visible on the stage.

```
when [flag] clicked
set TimeLeft ▼ to (20)
repeat (20)
    wait (1) seconds
    change TimeLeft ▼ by (-1)
broadcast Time's Up ▼
```

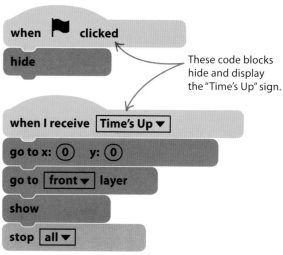

```
when [flag] clicked
hide

when I receive Time's Up ▼
go to x: (0)  y: (0)
go to front ▼ layer
show
stop all ▼
```

These code blocks hide and display the "Time's Up" sign.

▽ Mouse control

You could use a computer mouse as the controller for this game instead of the keyboard. The three blocks below allow you to set the launch angle and speed as well as make the monkey jump. See if you can figure out some code to use them.

Use this block to make the monkey jump.

`mouse down?`

`distance to (mouse-pointer ▼)`

This block could be used to set launch speed.

`point towards (mouse-pointer ▼)`

Use this block to set launch angle.

▷ Bouncing bananas

To make the game a bit harder, you could try changing the Bananas sprite code so that the bananas bounce up and down on the stage.

▷ Danger! Snake!

Add another challenge by creating an obstacle that gets in the monkey's way or maybe ends the game—perhaps a giant monkey-eating snake or spider?

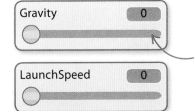

▽ Bug or bonus?

You might have discovered that you can adjust the monkey's speed in flight with the arrow keys. You can fix this by adding a new variable, "MonkeySpeed", and copying the value of "LaunchSpeed" into it at launch. Then use MonkeySpeed, not LaunchSpeed, in the move block for the monkey. Or if you enjoy being able to change the monkey's speed, leave the game as it is.

▽ Launch speed slider

You've already tried adding a slider to control gravity. You could also add a slider to adjust launch speed.

Gravity	0
○━━━━━━━━━	

Sliders let you change these variables using the mouse instead of the arrow keys.

LaunchSpeed	0
○━━━━━━━━━	

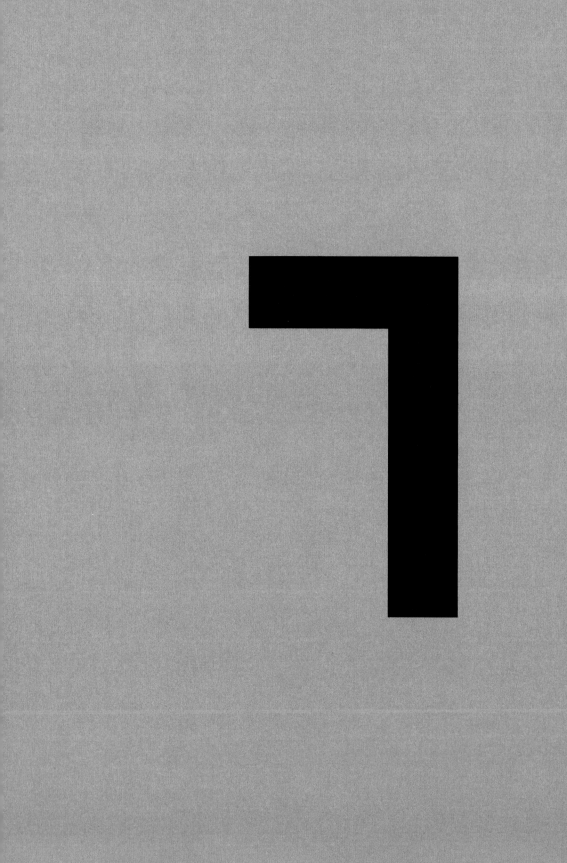

Doom on
the Broom

How to build Doom on the Broom

Games usually have a theme. This spooky game starts with a bat swooping in on the player, followed by scary ghosts and monsters. Get ready to bring these sprites to life with animation.

AIM OF THE GAME

The witch is out riding her broomstick in the forest when creatures of the night begin to advance on her from all sides. She must cast her fireball spell to dispose of the bats, ghosts, griffins, and dragons that would like to eat her for dinner.

◁ **Witch**
The witch sits in the center of the screen. Spin her broomstick with the arrow keys and cast fireballs with the space bar.

◁ **Enemies**
Every enemy hit by a fireball is destroyed and a point is scored. As you win points, the game speeds up.

◁ **Lives**
The witch loses a life if she is touched by any of her enemies. But if a flying hippo touches her, she wins an extra life.

Slow-moving ghosts drift in and fade away when hit.

Score   0

Super-fast griffins have a speedier attack.

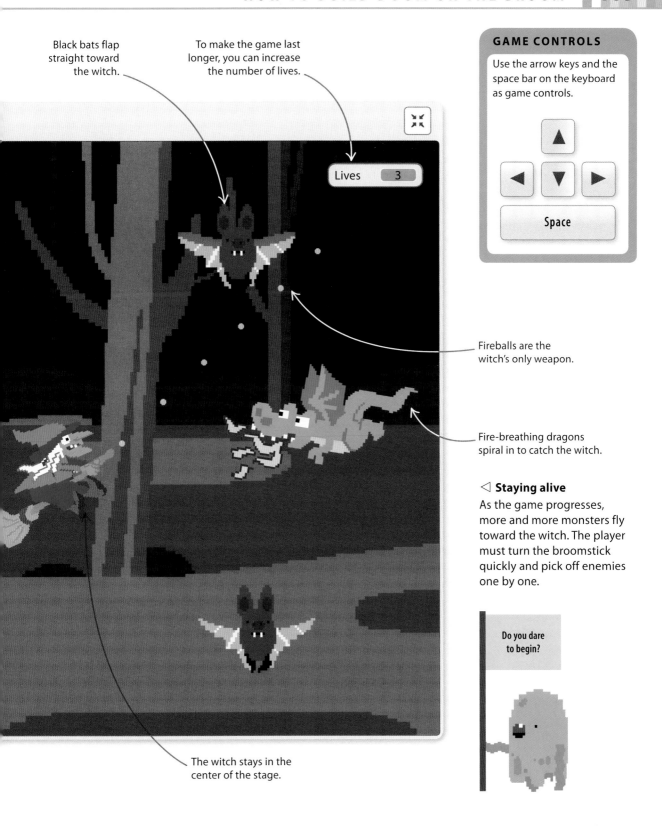

Black bats flap straight toward the witch.

To make the game last longer, you can increase the number of lives.

Lives 3

Fireballs are the witch's only weapon.

Fire-breathing dragons spiral in to catch the witch.

The witch stays in the center of the stage.

GAME CONTROLS

Use the arrow keys and the space bar on the keyboard as game controls.

▲

◀ ▼ ▶

Space

◁ **Staying alive**

As the game progresses, more and more monsters fly toward the witch. The player must turn the broomstick quickly and pick off enemies one by one.

Do you dare to begin?

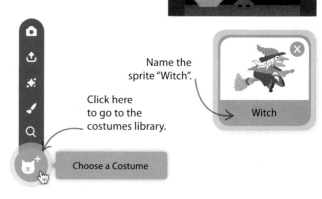

Setting the scene

Doom on the Broom has a spooky theme. The sprites, backdrop, and music are all chosen to create a certain atmosphere that draws the player into the game world. Start by putting together the Witch sprite, a dark forest, and some creepy music.

1 Start a new project and call it Doom on the Broom. Delete the cat sprite. Click the paint symbol 😺 in the sprites menu to create a blank sprite. Go to "Choose a Costume" and select the Witch costume from the costumes library. The costume will appear as a sprite in the sprites list.

Name the sprite "Witch".

Click here to go to the costumes library.

Choose a Costume

Witch

2 Click on the "Choose a Backdrop" symbol 🖼 and add the backdrop "Woods". This will lend an eerie setting to the game, which fits with the theme.

3 Load the sound "Cave" from the sound library and add this code to the stage's code area. Run the project and admire the spooky atmosphere you've created.

This block keeps the sound playing in a loop.

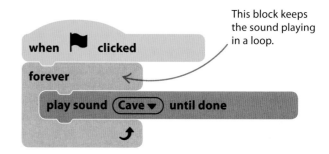

```
when 🏴 clicked
forever
    play sound (Cave ▼) until done
```

4 For extra creepiness, add this code to the stage to make it slowly but continually change color while the game is playing.

This block changes all the colors in the backdrop by a small amount each time it's run.

```
when 🏴 clicked
forever
    change [color ▼] effect by (1)
```

5 Now add the witch's first enemy: a sinister black bat. Open the sprites library and select Bat.

Bat

6 The bat looks scary but it doesn't move. Click the Costumes tab—you'll notice the bat has four different costumes. These costumes can be used to make the bat flap its wings. You only need two costumes—"bat-a" and "bat-b"—for this game. Delete the rest.

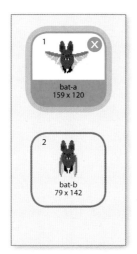

1

bat-a
159 x 120

2

bat-b
79 x 142

7 Add this code to the bat to make the costumes swap back and forth. Now run the project to see the bat flapping its wings.

when ⚑ clicked

forever

next costume

wait (0.1) seconds

This sets the flap speed of the bat.

■ ■ **GAME DESIGN**

Animation

You can make pictures appear to move by showing slightly different versions of the same picture one after another. This fools the brain into thinking that it is a single moving image. This is called animation, and it is how all cartoons work. Scratch lets you animate a sprite by rapidly changing costumes that show it in different poses. When these costumes appear one after the other, you can see flapping bats, walking cats, and jumping frogs.

Controlling the witch

Your spooky game is now starting to take shape, but you'll need to add some more code blocks to get things working. The following code lets the player take control of the witch.

8 Go to Variables in the blocks palette and then click "Make a Variable". Create the variables "Score", "Lives", and "GameSpeed". Show the variables "Score" and "Lives" on the stage. Add the following code to the witch to set things up and to control her with the arrow keys. Read the code carefully and test it to see if it works.

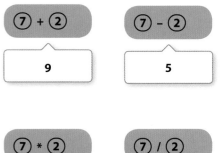

EXPERT TIPS

Arithmetic operators

Computer programmers have to use special symbols to do math. Almost every computer language uses * for multiply and / for divide because the usual symbols aren't on a computer keyboard. Look in the green Operators section for the arithmetic operators. Click on the blocks in the code area to see the answers appear in a speech bubble.

7 + 2	7 – 2
9	5

7 * 2	7 / 2
14	3.5

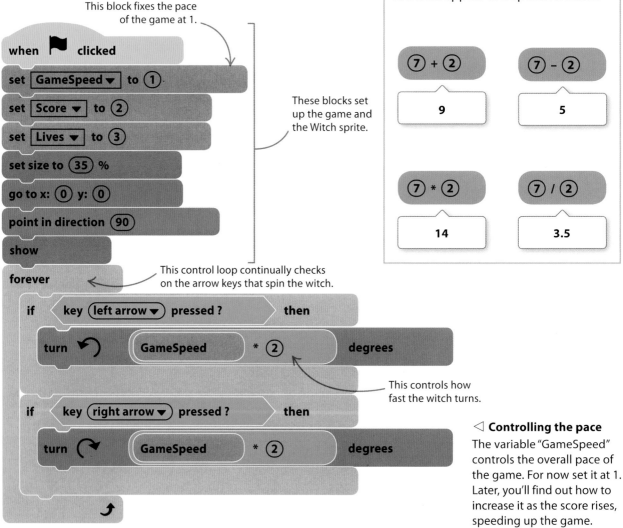

This block fixes the pace of the game at 1.

These blocks set up the game and the Witch sprite.

This control loop continually checks on the arrow keys that spin the witch.

This controls how fast the witch turns.

◁ **Controlling the pace**
The variable "GameSpeed" controls the overall pace of the game. For now set it at 1. Later, you'll find out how to increase it as the score rises, speeding up the game.

Casting fireballs

The witch's only defense against the rampaging spooks will be her fireball spell. The next bit of code will make a fireball shoot from her broomstick when the player presses the space bar.

9 Add the Ball sprite from the library and rename it "Fireball". It's currently too big, but you'll shrink it down in a moment.

Fireball

10 Add the following two code blocks to the Fireball sprite. Each fireball launched by the witch will be a clone of the sprite.

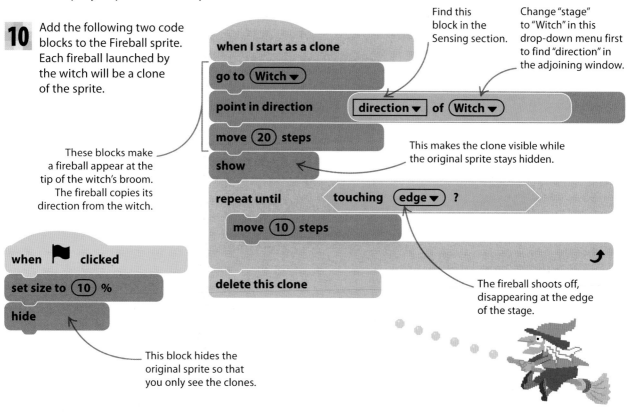

Find this block in the Sensing section.

Change "stage" to "Witch" in this drop-down menu first to find "direction" in the adjoining window.

```
when I start as a clone
go to (Witch ▼)
point in direction    direction ▼  of (Witch ▼)
move (20) steps
show
repeat until     touching (edge ▼) ?
    move (10) steps
delete this clone
```

These blocks make a fireball appear at the tip of the witch's broom. The fireball copies its direction from the witch.

This makes the clone visible while the original sprite stays hidden.

```
when ⚑ clicked
set size to (10) %
hide
```

This block hides the original sprite so that you only see the clones.

The fireball shoots off, disappearing at the edge of the stage.

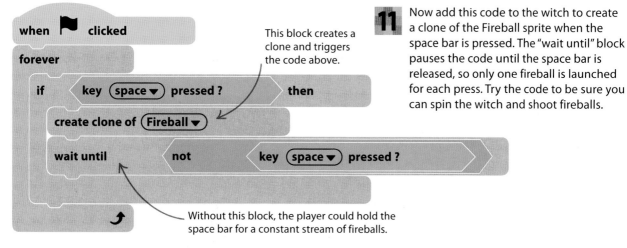

```
when ⚑ clicked
forever
    if    key (space ▼) pressed ?    then
        create clone of (Fireball ▼)
        wait until    not    key (space ▼) pressed ?
```

This block creates a clone and triggers the code above.

11 Now add this code to the witch to create a clone of the Fireball sprite when the space bar is pressed. The "wait until" block pauses the code until the space bar is released, so only one fireball is launched for each press. Try the code to be sure you can spin the witch and shoot fireballs.

Without this block, the player could hold the space bar for a constant stream of fireballs.

Bat attack

One flapping bat isn't going to scare a powerful spellcaster like the witch, but you can add clones to make a whole squadron of bats.

12 Add these two code blocks to the bat. They work together to create an endless supply of bats that advance toward the witch from random points around the edge of the stage.

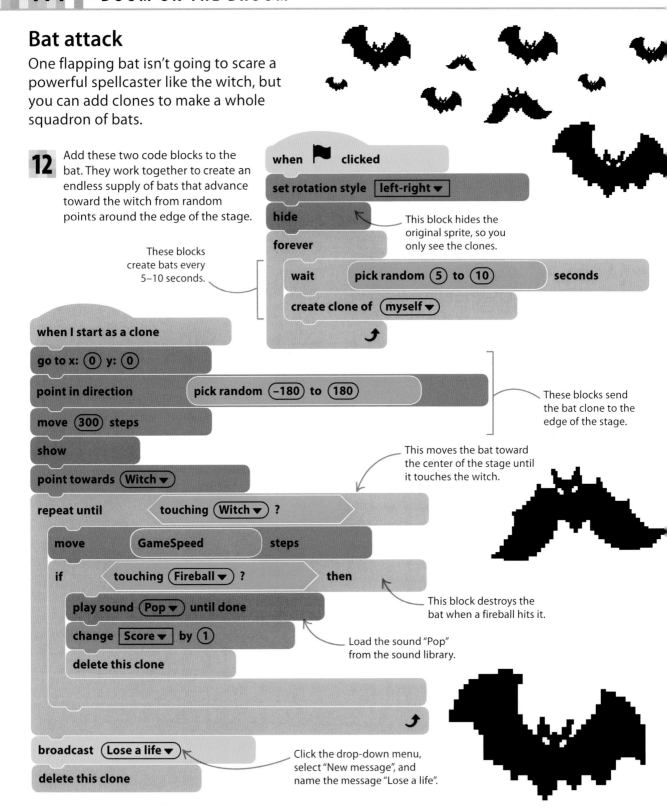

when ⚑ clicked

set rotation style [left-right ▼]

hide

This block hides the original sprite, so you only see the clones.

forever

These blocks create bats every 5–10 seconds.

wait (pick random (5) to (10)) seconds

create clone of (myself ▼)

when I start as a clone

go to x: (0) y: (0)

point in direction (pick random (-180) to (180))

These blocks send the bat clone to the edge of the stage.

move (300) steps

show

point towards (Witch ▼)

This moves the bat toward the center of the stage until it touches the witch.

repeat until < touching (Witch ▼) ? >

move (GameSpeed) steps

if < touching (Fireball ▼) ? > then

This block destroys the bat when a fireball hits it.

play sound (Pop ▼) until done

change [Score ▼] by (1)

Load the sound "Pop" from the sound library.

delete this clone

broadcast (Lose a life ▼)

Click the drop-down menu, select "New message", and name the message "Lose a life".

delete this clone

▷ **How does it work?**

The three blue Motion blocks at the start of the bat clone's code move the clone to a random point at the edge of the stage. The hidden clone first moves to the center and picks a random direction. Then it moves 300 steps—far enough to reach the edge in any direction. This way, bat clones will attack from every direction with equal chance. The witch doesn't touch the bat when it first moves to the center, because you can't touch a hidden sprite.

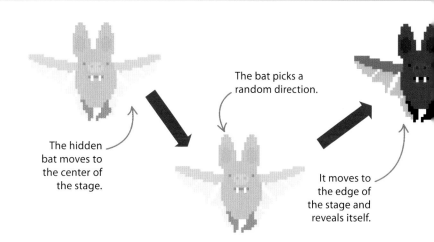

The bat picks a random direction.

The hidden bat moves to the center of the stage.

It moves to the edge of the stage and reveals itself.

13 It's a good idea to remove all the bats whenever the witch loses a life. This gives her a chance to recover before the next wave of attackers. Add this code to the bat to do the job. When the message "Lose a life" is received, every clone runs the code and all the bats disappear.

14 Run the project to see if it works. A bat should appear after a few seconds and will move toward the witch. Soon more will appear. The witch should be able to use her fireballs to destroy them. All the bats will disappear when one finally reaches the witch.

```
when I receive  Lose a life ▼
delete this clone
```

15 You might notice that the bats aren't flapping anymore. To fix this, adjust the code below so that it runs for each clone instead of just the original sprite.

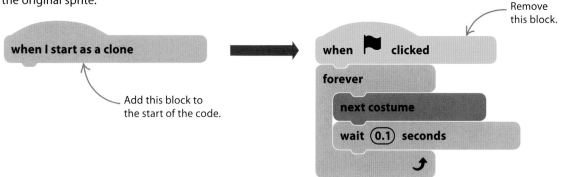

```
when I start as a clone
```

Add this block to the start of the code.

Remove this block.

```
when 🏳 clicked
forever
  next costume
  wait 0.1 seconds
```

Adding explosions

Not much happens when the witch loses a life. Fix this to make the witch go out with a bang by creating some fireworks, adding a scream, and updating the counter that shows how many lives she has left.

16 Add this code to the witch to make her react to losing a life. If she still has lives left, she will disappear for two seconds before returning to battle. If she's out of lives, then it's game over. Add a new message, "GameOver", which you'll need later in the project. Now try the game again. The witch should lose lives and stop completely when the "Lives" variable has a value of 0.

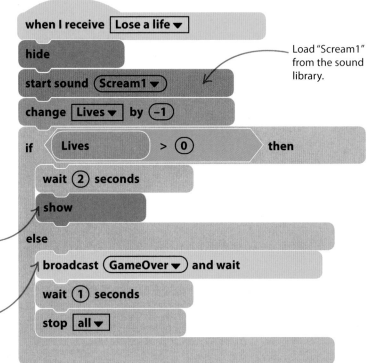

Load "Scream1" from the sound library.

This makes the witch reappear after a pause if she has any lives left.

The "GameOver" message will trigger a sign that you'll create later.

17 To create fireworks you need a new sprite. Load another Ball sprite from the sprites library instead of copying the Fireball sprite. Rename this new sprite "Explosion" and then click on the Costumes tab. Select the second costume so that the ball turns blue.

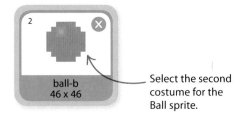

ball-b
46 x 46

Select the second costume for the Ball sprite.

18 Now add these two code blocks to the Explosion sprite. The first bit of code creates 72 tiny, hidden blue ball clones, all pointing in different directions. The second bit of code makes them fly out in a circle from the witch's location. Read the code blocks carefully and try to figure out what triggers the explosion.

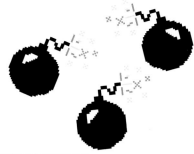

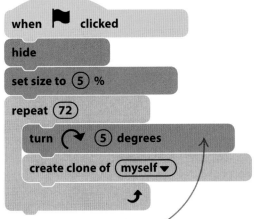

This makes each clone point in a different direction.

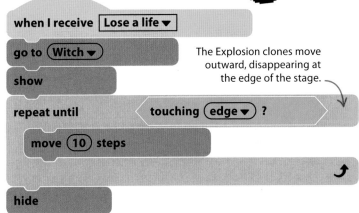

The Explosion clones move outward, disappearing at the edge of the stage.

Move the Lives tab to the top right of the window.

19 When the Explosion sprite receives the message "Lose a life", all the blue ball clones appear at the witch's location and explode out to the edge of the stage before hiding once again. Run the game and let a bat reach the witch to check how it works.

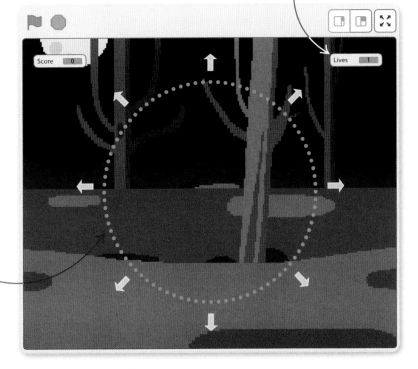

When a bat touches the witch, she explodes into a circle of flying blue balls.

Speedy specter

It's now time to increase the fear factor and add a different sprite to the game. You can copy the existing black bat, and add new costumes and alter the code blocks to create a super-fast griffin.

20 To avoid having to rebuild all the code from the black bat, simply right-click it and create a copy by selecting "duplicate". A sprite named Bat2 will appear in the sprites list. Rename it "Fast griffin".

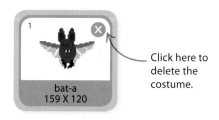

Click here to copy the sprite.

21 Click on Fast griffin's Costumes tab—you'll see the copied black bat's two costumes. To make Fast griffin look different from the black bat, you need to load some new costumes. Click on the symbol 🐱 at the bottom left of the Scratch window to choose a new costume from the library.

Click here to add new costumes.

Use costumes to change our looks, expressions, or posture.

22 Add the two new costumes, "Griffin-a" and "Griffin-b". They show a griffin with wings in two different positions.

23 Now delete the unnecessary black bat costumes in this sprite. To do this, select the costume you want to delete and then click the small "x" in the top right.

Click here to delete the costume.

24 To speed up the fast griffin, change its "move" block to make the griffin move twice as fast as the black bat.

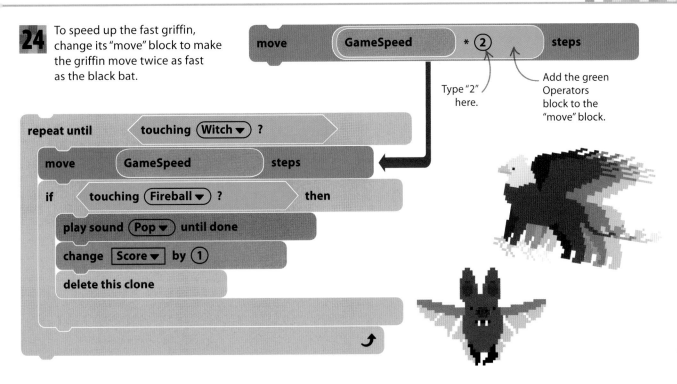

move (GameSpeed * ②) steps

Type "2" here.

Add the green Operators block to the "move" block.

repeat until (touching (Witch ▼) ?)

   move (GameSpeed) steps

   if (touching (Fireball ▼) ?) then

      play sound (Pop ▼) until done

      change (Score ▼) by ①

      delete this clone

25 The game would be too hard with lots of fast griffins, so make the following changes to the existing code to make them appear later in the game and less frequently.

26 Check that you have four code blocks in Fast griffin's code area, just like in Bat. Run the game. After a few black bats have attacked, a faster, much more dangerous griffin will appear, flapping away.

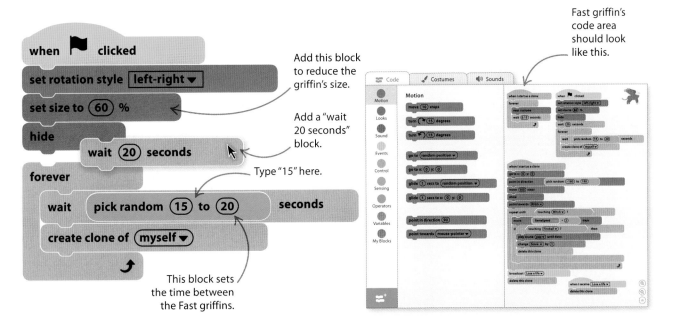

when 🏳 clicked

set rotation style [left-right ▼]

set size to ⑥⓪ %

hide

   wait ⑳ seconds

forever

   wait (pick random ⑮ to ⑳) seconds

   create clone of (myself ▼)

Add this block to reduce the griffin's size.

Add a "wait 20 seconds" block.

Type "15" here.

This block sets the time between the Fast griffins.

Fast griffin's code area should look like this.

Fire-breathing dragon

The witch's next enemy is a fire-breathing dragon. Instead of flapping straight toward the witch as the bats and griffins do, it will spiral in slowly, which gives her more time to defend herself.

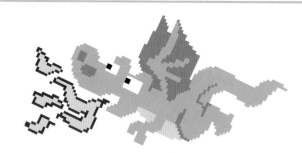

27 Copy the Bat sprite again, but rename it "Dragon". Load the two new costumes "Dragon1-a" and "Dragon1-b", then delete the two bat costumes.

Dragon

Type the new sprite's name here.

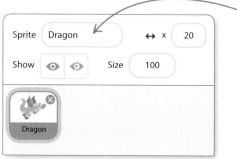

| Sprite | Dragon | | ↔ x | 20 |
| Show | 👁 👁 | | Size | 100 |

Dragon

28 Now make a few changes to the code blocks in the copied sprite. First, change the costume code to make the dragon breathe fire in short bursts.

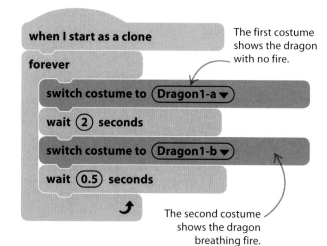

```
when I start as a clone
forever
    switch costume to (Dragon1-a ▼)
    wait (2) seconds
    switch costume to (Dragon1-b ▼)
    wait (0.5) seconds
```

The first costume shows the dragon with no fire.

The second costume shows the dragon breathing fire.

29 Next, modify the dragon's movement to make it fly in a spiral path by moving the "point towards Witch" block into the "repeat until" loop and adding a "turn right 80 degrees" block.

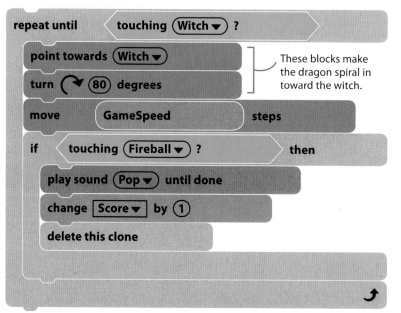

```
repeat until < touching (Witch ▼) ? >
    point towards (Witch ▼)
    turn ↻ (80) degrees
    move ( GameSpeed ) steps
    if < touching (Fireball ▼) ? > then
        play sound (Pop ▼) until done
        change (Score ▼) by (1)
        delete this clone
```

These blocks make the dragon spiral in toward the witch.

30 Add a "wait 10 seconds" block to the main code to delay the dragon's arrival on the stage. Then change the numbers in the "pick random" block to "10" and "15". This will make a clone of the dragon appear every 10–15 seconds. Once you've made all the changes, test the game to see if it works.

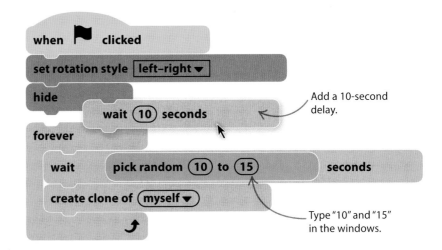

Add a 10-second delay.

Type "10" and "15" in the windows.

• • • **GAME DESIGN**

Working with themes

In Doom on the Broom, spooky scenery and supernatural characters work together to give the game a theme. A strong theme that ties together the elements of a game can make it feel polished and professional. Working with themes is also great fun because you can let your imagination run wild.

△ **Story**

A background story or quest helps give a game a theme. Perhaps the player is trying to escape a haunted house, search for underwater treasure, or explore an alien planet. Instead of inventing a story, you can use a well-known one, but give it a twist, such as putting Goldilocks and the three bears in space.

△ **Music and sound effects**

Sounds in a game have a big influence on how the player feels. Spooky music makes the player nervous, but happy music makes a game feel cheerful, even if the pictures are spooky. Choose sound effects carefully so they match the sprite or situation that triggers them.

△ **Scenery**

If you choose the right backdrop, sprites in the game will look like they are really there instead of stuck on top. You can create your own backdrops in Scratch's paint editor, but you can also upload images you've found or created elsewhere.

△ **Sprites**

The player is usually the hero in a game, so choose a likable sprite. The enemies don't have to look scary—even cute sprites can seem scary when they attack. If players have to collect objects, make them look valuable, such as coins or gems.

Ghost

Supernatural heroes should have supernatural enemies, so add some ghosts to chase the witch. Instead of vanishing when fireballs hit them, the ghosts will fade away.

31 To create the ghost, make a copy of the Bat sprite again. Rename the new sprite "Ghost" and replace the Bat costumes with "Ghost-a" and "Ghost-b".

32 Modify the code below so that the costumes change every second.

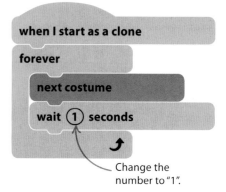

when I start as a clone
forever
  next costume
  wait (1) seconds

Change the number to "1".

33 Change the ghost's code so that it moves slowly and fades out when hit by a fireball. Click the Sounds tab above the blocks palette and load the "Screech" sound from the sound library. Then change the selection in the "start sound" block to "Screech" to make the ghost scream when it vanishes.

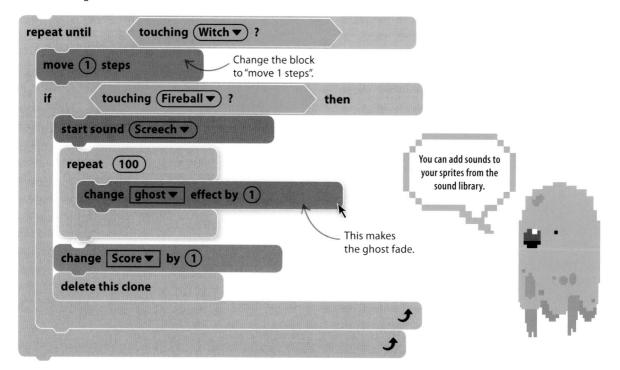

repeat until < touching (Witch) ? >
  move (1) steps
  if < touching (Fireball) ? > then
    start sound (Screech)
    repeat (100)
      change [ghost] effect by (1)
    change [Score] by (1)
    delete this clone

Change the block to "move 1 steps".

This makes the ghost fade.

You can add sounds to your sprites from the sound library.

34 Now add a "wait 10 seconds" block to the main code to delay the ghost's first appearance. Change the numbers in the "pick random" block to make ghosts appear more often than bats.

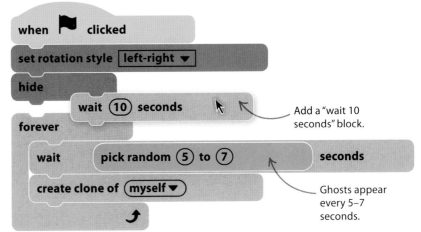

when ⚑ clicked

set rotation style [left-right ▼]

hide

wait (10) seconds

Add a "wait 10 seconds" block.

forever

wait pick random (5) to (7) seconds

Ghosts appear every 5–7 seconds.

create clone of (myself ▼)

35 Once all of your changes are complete, test the game. Try fireballing each enemy to make sure the code works.

Score 30

The ghost should slowly fade when hit with a fireball.

36 You can go to the Scratch library and add more monsters to your game. Remember to copy the Bat sprite and replace its costumes with new ones to avoid having to rebuild the code from the beginning. Update the new monster's code to use the new costumes and adjust the timings.

Finishing touches

It's time to add some finishing touches to the game. To make it look more professional, add a game-over screen that appears when the witch runs out of lives. You can also program the witch to give instructions to the players at the start of the game.

37 Click on the paintbrush symbol ✎ in the sprites list to create a new sprite in the paint editor. Using "Convert to Bitmap", draw a rectangle and fill it with a dark color. Now switch to "Convert to Vector". Click on the text tool, choose a font you like, and select red for the text color. Click in the rectangle and type GAME OVER! and use the selection tool to make the text large.

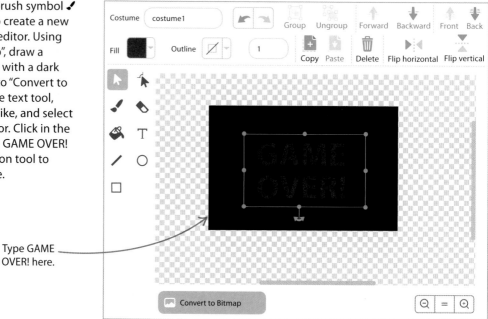

Type GAME OVER! here.

38 Now add these code blocks to the new sprite to hide it at the start and show it only at the end when the witch loses all her lives. Run the game. Once the witch loses all her lives, the message will be displayed on the stage.

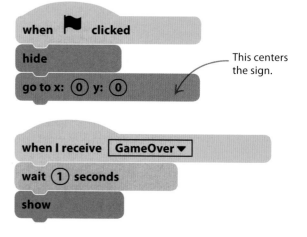

```
when 🏳 clicked
hide
go to x: 0 y: 0
```

This centers the sign.

```
when I receive GameOver ▼
wait 1 seconds
show
```

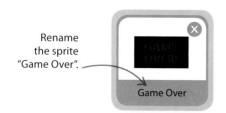

Rename the sprite "Game Over".

Game Over

39 Add this code to the witch so that she gives instructions to the player at the start of the game. You can change the three seconds in the "say" block if it's too quick, but not for too long—those bats won't wait.

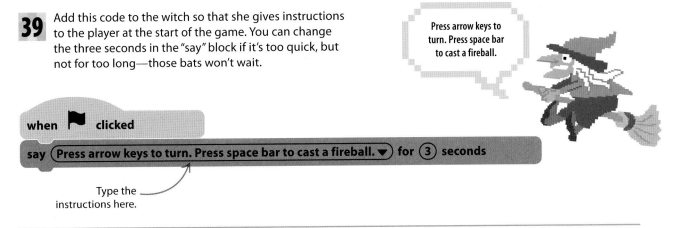

Type the instructions here.

Challenger mode

As players become more skilled and score more points, they may start to get bored with the game. You can prevent this by making the game faster as it progresses.

40 To make the game speed up as the player scores points, add a block inside the witch's movement loop that sets the "GameSpeed" variable using the variable "Score".

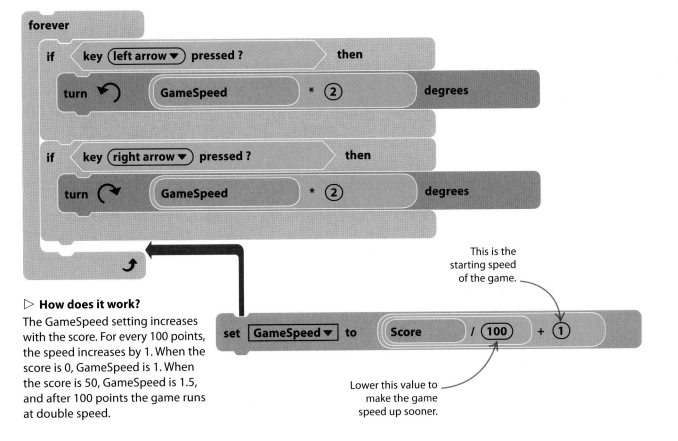

This is the starting speed of the game.

Lower this value to make the game speed up sooner.

▷ **How does it work?**
The GameSpeed setting increases with the score. For every 100 points, the speed increases by 1. When the score is 0, GameSpeed is 1. When the score is 50, GameSpeed is 1.5, and after 100 points the game runs at double speed.

Extra lives hippo

So far you've mainly added enemies. To help the player, add a friendly flying hippo that gives the witch extra lives if it reaches her without getting hit by a fireball.

41 Copy the Bat sprite, but replace its costumes with two copies of Hippo1-b. Use the paint editor to write the messages EXTRA LIFE and DON'T FIREBALL ME! on the costumes so the player knows it isn't an enemy. Rename the sprite "Hippo".

42 Amend the code blocks so that instead of gaining a point when you fireball the hippo, you earn an extra life when it touches you. Change the value in the "point in direction" block so the text on the hippo doesn't get reversed.

Change this value to "0".

```
point in direction    pick random (-180) to (0)
move (300) steps
show
point towards (Witch ▾)
repeat until      touching (Witch ▾) ?
    move    GameSpeed    steps
    if      touching (Fireball ▾) ?    then
        play sound (Pop ▾) until done
        delete this clone
change [Lives ▾] by (1)
delete this clone
```

This block adds an extra life to the Witch sprite's lives counter.

43 Change the wait time in the costume code so that the hippo swaps costumes once a second, giving players time to read the signs.

```
when I start as a clone
forever
    next costume
    wait (1) seconds
```

This makes the hippo alternate between its two costumes every second.

44 To avoid making the game too easy, make the extra lives hippos rare. Change this code so they appear only every 30–60 seconds.

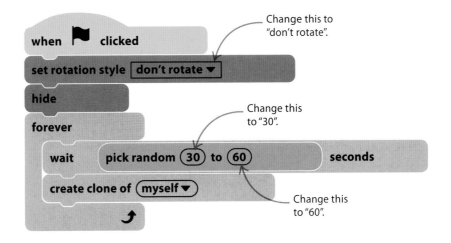

when ⚑ clicked

set rotation style don't rotate ▼

Change this to "don't rotate".

hide

forever

wait pick random 30 to 60 seconds

Change this to "30".

create clone of myself ▼

Change this to "60".

Hacks and tweaks

Now that your game works, you can experiment and make it your own by changing and adding elements. Try these suggestions to get started.

▷ **Flying Witch**
You can make the witch fly instead of rotating on the spot by adding the code shown here. To make her turn faster while flying, increase the numbers in her "turn" blocks.

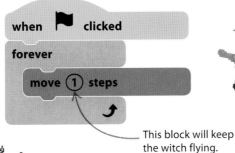

when ⚑ clicked

forever

move 1 steps

This block will keep the witch flying.

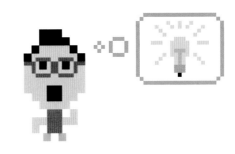

△ **Spell binder**
Can you think of another spell that the witch can cast? Tweak her code and costumes so she strikes her enemies with lightning, or make her cast some other fancy spells.

▷ **Mouse control**
Use this code to let the player spin the witch with a mouse instead of the keyboard. If the game is too easy, increase the GameSpeed value. You can also try changing the code so the computer mouse casts the fireballs.

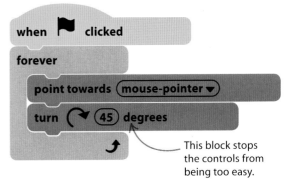

when ⚑ clicked

forever

point towards mouse-pointer ▼

turn ↻ 45 degrees

This block stops the controls from being too easy.

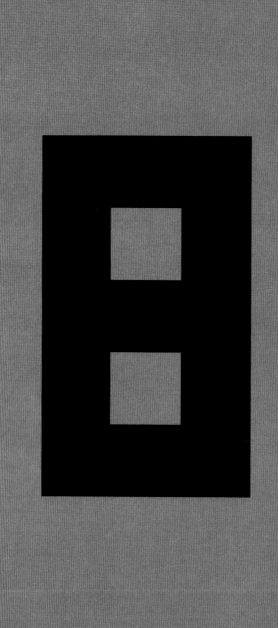

Dog's Dinner

How to build Dog's Dinner

Dog's Dinner is a platform game. In this type of game, the player's character jumps from platform to platform collecting goodies and avoiding enemies and traps. The key to success is timing your jumps perfectly so you stay in the game.

AIM OF THE GAME

The dog likes bones but hates junk food. Steer him through three levels, jumping from platform to platform. Collect all the tasty bones on the stage and then go through the portal to the next level. But make sure he avoids the unhealthy cakes, cheese puffs, and donuts!

◁ **Dog**
Use the left and right arrow keys to make the dog run. When he needs to jump, press the space bar.

◁ **Bones**
You need to collect all the bones to open the portal to the next level. It will remain shut until you have them all.

◁ **Junk food**
If the dog touches any junk food, it's game over and you have to start again on Level 1—no matter which level you were on!

The dog runs and jumps around the level. He can jump only when he's standing on a platform.

Collect all the bones—you can't get through the portal without them.

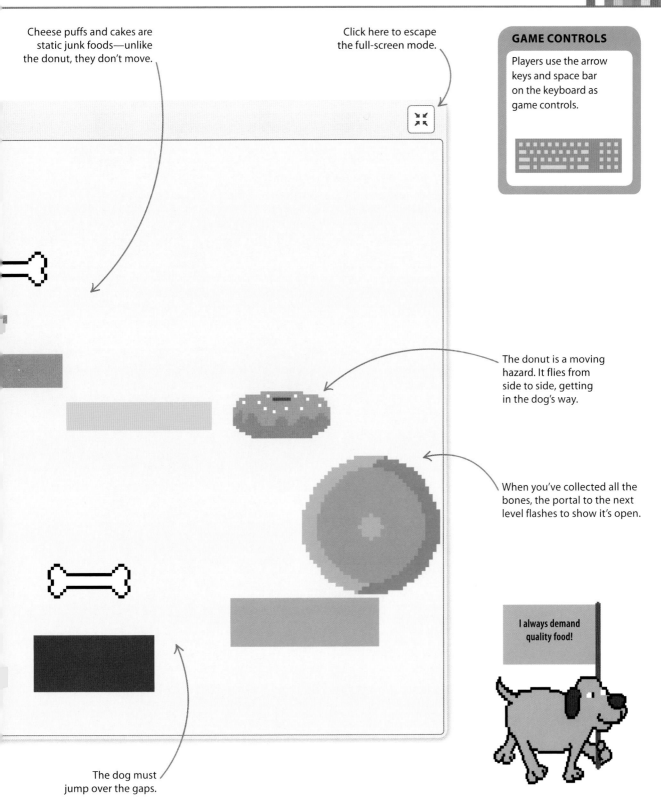

Cheese puffs and cakes are static junk foods—unlike the donut, they don't move.

Click here to escape the full-screen mode.

GAME CONTROLS

Players use the arrow keys and space bar on the keyboard as game controls.

The donut is a moving hazard. It flies from side to side, getting in the dog's way.

When you've collected all the bones, the portal to the next level flashes to show it's open.

I always demand quality food!

The dog must jump over the gaps.

Player on a platform

This is a complicated game, so you'll need to check your work carefully at every stage. But don't worry, the project builds gradually, one step at a time. Start by getting a very simple player sprite to work properly with a platform. At first, the player is just a red square. This makes it easy to sense collisions with the platforms. You can add the blue dog on top of it later.

At last I'm going to be a star!

1 Create a new project and name it "Dog's Dinner". To make your simple player, click the paintbrush symbol in the sprites menu. Make sure you select "Convert to Bitmap". Choose red from the color palette in the paint editor, select the rectangle tool, and click on the filled square option.

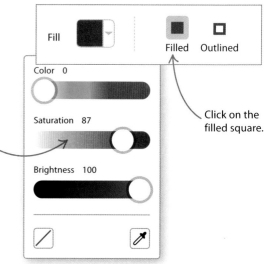

Fill | Filled | Outlined

Color 0

Saturation 87

Brightness 100

Click on the filled square.

Choose red from the palette.

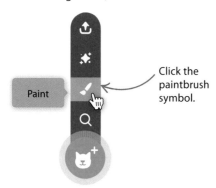

Paint

Click the paintbrush symbol.

2 Hold down the shift key and drag the mouse-pointer over the painting area to draw a small red square. If you click outside your block and look at the list of costumes, you'll see the size of the square; aim for 35 x 35.

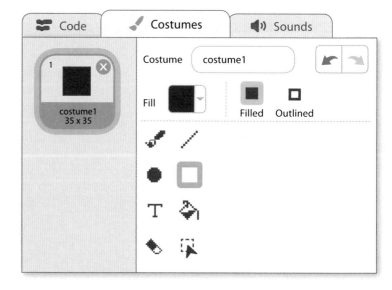

Code | Costumes | Sounds

1

costume1
35 x 35

Costume costume1

Fill | Filled | Outlined

The block should be smaller than the cat's face on the stage.

3 You can resize your block if it's too big or too small. Using the "Select" tool, click and drag to draw a square around the block. Use the corner points to resize it. Do this until the size is right. Make sure the square overlaps the small cross in the middle of the painting area.

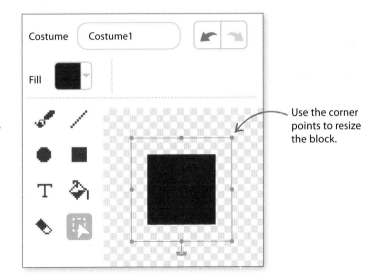

Use the corner points to resize the block.

4 Rename the sprite "PlayerBlock". Your player sprite is done. Now you can delete the cat sprite.

We don't need you for this game, Cat, so we're deleting you.

Yes, I know ... but I'll be back!

5 Now add a simple platform. Click the paintbrush symbol in the sprites menu again to create a new sprite. Use the rectangle tool to draw a floor with two obstacle blocks on top. Call this sprite "Platforms". On the stage, drag your PlayerBlock and place it between the obstacles, but make sure it's not touching the platform.

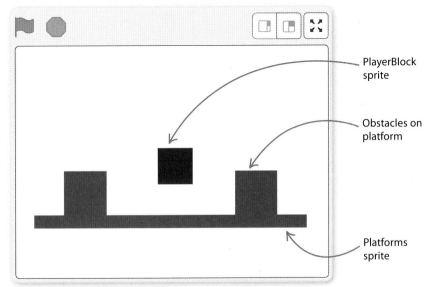

PlayerBlock sprite

Obstacles on platform

Platforms sprite

Running around

The next step is to make the PlayerBlock run when the player presses the arrow keys. You'll need some code that will keep it from running through obstacles by making it reverse when it touches them. To make the code easier to read, you'll be making your own customized Scratch blocks.

6 With the PlayerBlock sprite selected, go to the blocks palette under the Code tab and click on My Blocks.

7 There are no blocks in this section yet, only some buttons. Click on the "Make a Block" button. Type "Run controls" in the window that opens to name your new block and then click "OK".

Type the name of your new block here.

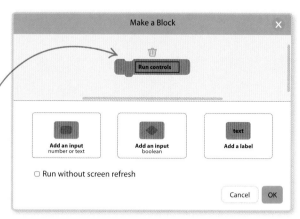

8 The new block appears in the My Blocks section, and a special pink "define" header block appears in the code area.

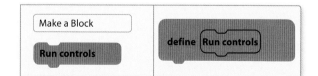

Subprograms

Scratch lets you group together blocks under a "define" header block and run them by using a new block that you name. This saves you from building the same group of blocks again if you want to use it in more than one place. (However, the new block will work only with the sprite that you created it for.) Giving your new block a meaningful name will make your code easy to understand. Most programming languages let you take some useful code, give it a name, and wrap it up as a unit. Different languages call these units different things: subprograms, subroutines, procedures, and functions are some common names.

I love using these subprogram blocks!

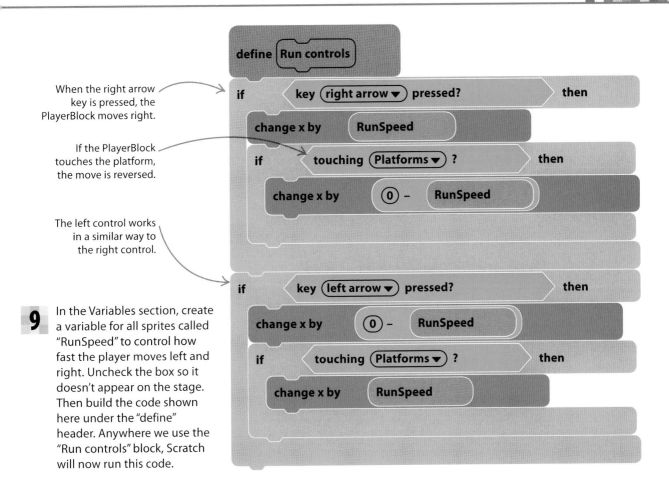

When the right arrow key is pressed, the PlayerBlock moves right.

If the PlayerBlock touches the platform, the move is reversed.

The left control works in a similar way to the right control.

9 In the Variables section, create a variable for all sprites called "RunSpeed" to control how fast the player moves left and right. Uncheck the box so it doesn't appear on the stage. Then build the code shown here under the "define" header. Anywhere we use the "Run controls" block, Scratch will now run this code.

10 Next, add the code below to use your new custom block in a "forever" loop.

11 Now run the project. You should be able to move the red block left and right with the arrow keys, but not be able to move through the obstacles.

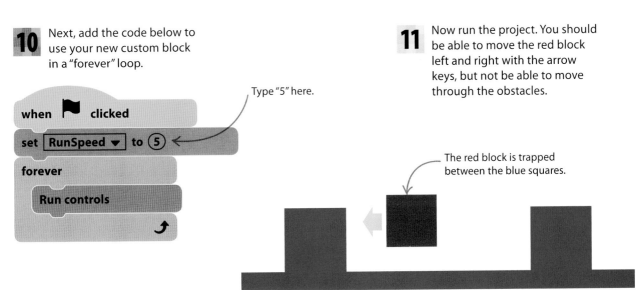

Type "5" here.

The red block is trapped between the blue squares.

Up and down

Platform games are all about jumping. You can't jump without gravity, so you need to add some simulated gravity to the game. You may recognize how the simulated gravity works if you built the Jumpy Monkey game.

12 Add two more variables for all sprites: "Gravity" and "FallSpeed". Uncheck both boxes. Then click on My Blocks and make a new block called "Simulate gravity", following the code shown here. It moves the PlayerBlock down by the amount "FallSpeed" and then checks to see if the PlayerBlock has hit the platforms. If so, it reverses the last move and sets "FallSpeed" to zero so that the platform stops the player's fall.

When "FallSpeed" is negative, the PlayerBlock falls.

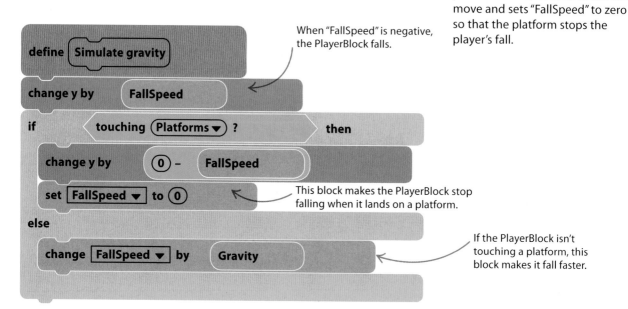

This block makes the PlayerBlock stop falling when it lands on a platform.

If the PlayerBlock isn't touching a platform, this block makes it fall faster.

You need to set the value of gravity!

13 Insert the blocks shown here into the PlayerBlock's main code. Make sure you set the value of "Gravity" to "–1" and set FallSpeed to "0".

Insert "set Gravity to" and "set Fallspeed to" here.

Put "Simulate gravity" into the "forever" loop.

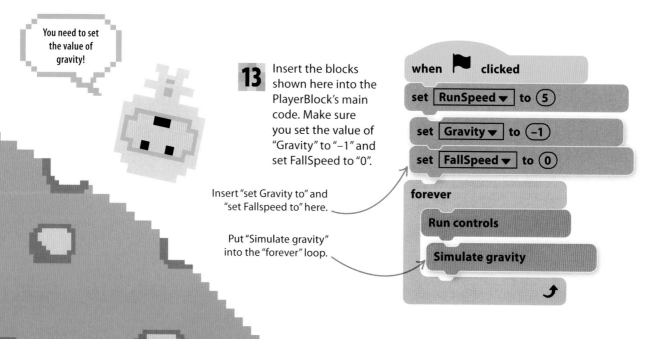

14 Run the project. Grab the red square with the mouse and drop it from above the platform. It will fall down and come to rest on the platform. But there's a problem: it slows down just above the platform. That's because our method makes the block reverse after hitting the platform and then start falling again at a slower speed. We can fix that later.

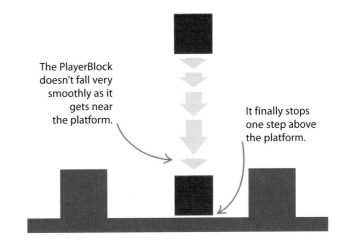

The PlayerBlock doesn't fall very smoothly as it gets near the platform.

It finally stops one step above the platform.

15 Now to create the jump. It's really easy: just add some new code to give the PlayerBlock an upward kick when you press the space bar. First, make a new variable for all sprites called "TakeoffSpeed". This is the player's upward speed on a jump. Then create a new block called "Jump control" and define it as shown here.

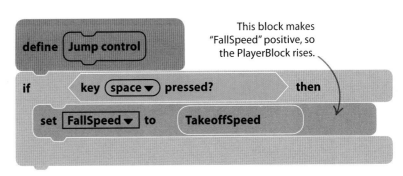

This block makes "FallSpeed" positive, so the PlayerBlock rises.

```
define  Jump control

if      key (space ▼) pressed?      then
    set  FallSpeed ▼  to  TakeoffSpeed
```

Insert "set TakeoffSpeed to" here.

```
when 🏴 clicked

set  TakeoffSpeed ▼  to (12)
set  RunSpeed ▼  to (5)
set  Gravity ▼  to (-1)
set  FallSpeed ▼  to (0)
forever
    Run controls
    Jump control
    Simulate gravity
```

16 Add the "set TakeoffSpeed to" block into the PlayerBlock's main code and set it to "12". Insert the "Jump control" block into the "forever" loop.

What happened there?

I think he forgot to set his takeoff speed!

Put "Jump control" into the "forever" loop.

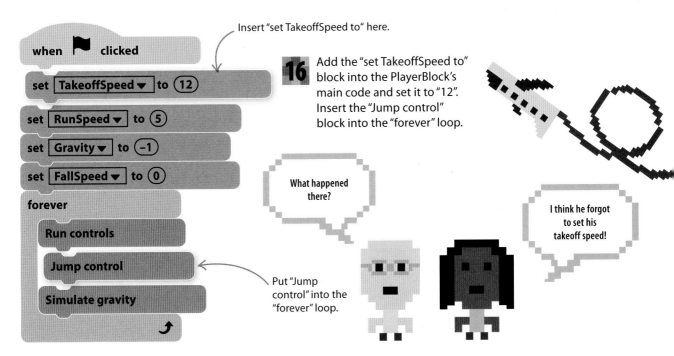

17 Now run the project. Press the space bar briefly. The PlayerBlock jumps up and comes back down again. You should be able to combine the run and jump controls to jump onto or over the obstacles on the platform. You now have the makings of a platform game! However, there's another bug: if you keep the space bar pressed, the PlayerBlock goes up forever.

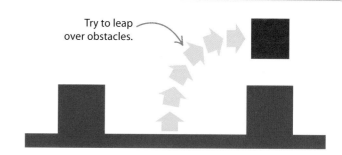

Try to leap over obstacles.

Fixing the jumping bugs

There are two bugs that spoil our jumps: one causes the PlayerBlock to jump infinitely high; the other keeps it from falling smoothly. You can fix them by tweaking the jump and gravity controls.

18 To fix the infinite jump bug, add a test to the "Jump control" code to check whether the player is on or just above the platform. (Remember that the "Simulate gravity" code leaves the PlayerBlock one step above the platform, so the two sprites aren't touching.) This fix will disable the space bar when the player is in mid-jump.

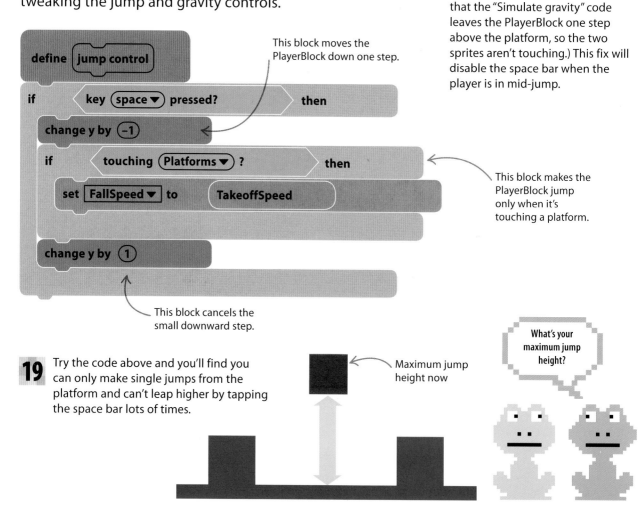

This block moves the PlayerBlock down one step.

This block makes the PlayerBlock jump only when it's touching a platform.

This block cancels the small downward step.

19 Try the code above and you'll find you can only make single jumps from the platform and can't leap higher by tapping the space bar lots of times.

Maximum jump height now

What's your maximum jump height?

20 To fix the other jumping bug (pausing just above the platform and then falling slowly again), you need to change what happens when the PlayerBlock touches the platform. At the moment, the red square reverses by the whole "FallSpeed" number when it hits a platform. Instead, we'll make it reverse in tiny steps until it's just above the platform. Create a new variable called "ReverseStep" for all sprites. Change the "define Simulate gravity" code as shown here.

This "if then else" block figures out which way the PlayerBlock needs to reverse.

If the PlayerBlock is falling ("FallSpeed" is negative), "ReverseStep" is set to +1 (up).

If the PlayerBlock is rising or stationary, "ReverseStep" is set to −1 (down).

The red square reverses by 1 step.

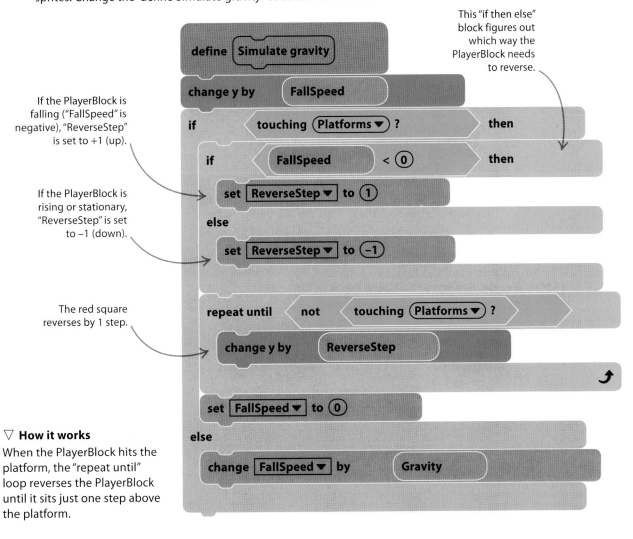

▽ **How it works**
When the PlayerBlock hits the platform, the "repeat until" loop reverses the PlayerBlock until it sits just one step above the platform.

The PlayerBlock lands inside the platform.

It reverses in single steps until it's just above the platform.

21 Try the jump again to see for yourself. You'll notice that the PlayerBlock rises back out of the platform very slowly. But we don't want that part to happen in slow motion! Scratch has a trick to fix this. Right-click on the "define Simulate gravity" header block and select "Edit" from the drop-down menu that appears.

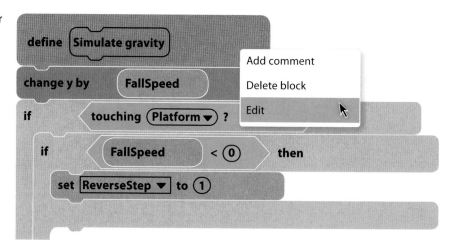

22 The "Make a Block" box appears again. Check "Run without screen refresh". This will make the gravity code run continually (without showing each reverse step), which will get rid of the slow-motion effect.

Check this box to make the code run much faster.

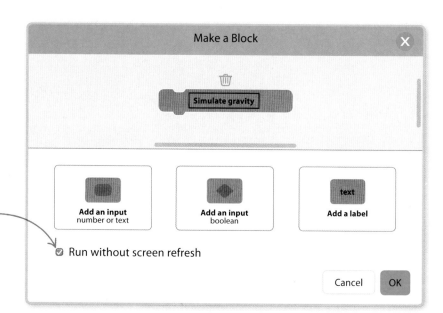

23 Now try jumping again. The tweaks you've made should help the PlayerBlock jump and land very smoothly.

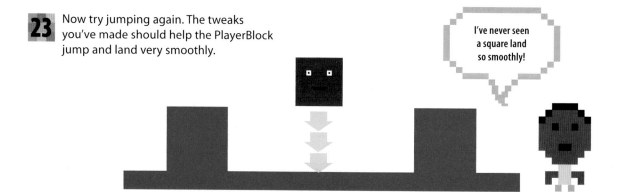

I've never seen a square land so smoothly!

GAME DESIGN

Which jump?

Games use many different types of jumps. Which type you choose is key to your game's design. Here are three common jumps.

▽ **Single jump**
This is the jump you have in Dog's Dinner—you can jump only if you're on the ground. You go up and then down, but in some games you can steer left and right during the jump.

▽ **Double jump**
This is the jump you had before you fixed the infinite jumping bug—you can jump again in the air to go higher. In some games there are limits on double jumping—for example, you can only do it if you're going up.

▽ **Wall jump**
When you touch a wall, you can jump up again. Ninja-type characters often have this power. It's not very realistic, but it's lots of fun!

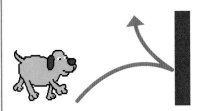

Falling off the level

Platform games are all about staying on the platforms. Add the next bit of code to the PlayerBlock to make the game end if it falls to the bottom of the stage.

24 Make a new block called "Fallen off", shown below, to check whether the PlayerBlock is at the bottom of the stage. Add it to the "forever" loop. Then build the short bit of code at the bottom of the page to stop the sprite when it gets the "GameOver" message. Test the new code: the controls should stop working when you hit the deck.

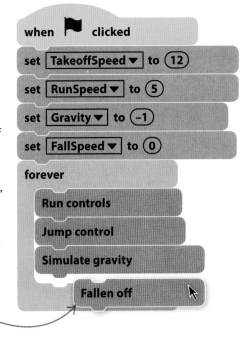

Drop this block inside the "forever" block.

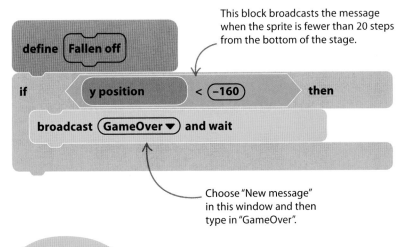

This block broadcasts the message when the sprite is fewer than 20 steps from the bottom of the stage.

Choose "New message" in this window and then type in "GameOver".

The "stop" block prevents the player from moving any farther.

Adding a character

A red square isn't a very interesting main character for a platform game. You need something fun that you can animate. It's time to introduce the dog.

Time for me to disappear!

This block makes the dog face to the right at the start.

```
when 🏳 clicked
set rotation style [left-right ▼]
set size to (50) %
point in direction (90)
show
forever
    go to (PlayerBlock ▼)
    go to [front ▼] layer
    if < key (left arrow ▼) pressed? > then
        point in direction (-90)
        next costume
    if < key (right arrow ▼) pressed? > then
        point in direction (90)
        next costume
```

The "go to" block places the dog on the red square.

The dog appears in front of the red square.

The dog faces left if the left arrow key is pressed.

The "next costume" blocks animate the dog's walk.

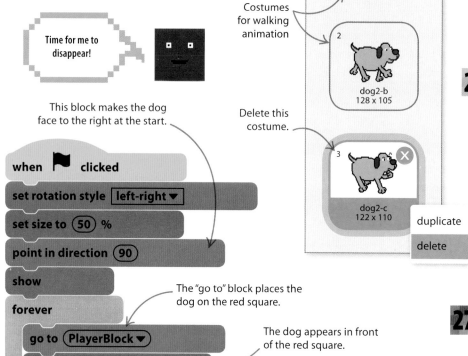

Costumes for walking animation

dog2-a
128 x 111

dog2-b
128 x 105

Delete this costume.

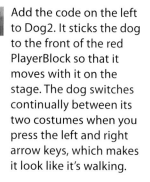

dog2-c
122 x 110

duplicate

delete

25 Click the sprite symbol in the sprites list to add a new sprite from the library. Select Dog2. This is a great sprite to use as it has more than one costume, which means you can animate it.

26 You need only Dog2's first two costumes for now, so go to the Costumes tab and delete the last costume (dog2-c).

27 Add the code on the left to Dog2. It sticks the dog to the front of the red PlayerBlock so that it moves with it on the stage. The dog switches continually between its two costumes when you press the left and right arrow keys, which makes it look like it's walking.

Look— I'm walking!

You can shift the dog up or down on the platform by moving the center of the PlayerBlock sprite.

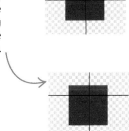

28 Run the project—the dog will now run around the stage with the PlayerBlock. If its paws are too low down on the platform, you can raise the center point of the PlayerBlock costume in the paint editor (since the dog sticks itself to the PlayerBlock). The dog is just decoration, so it doesn't really matter if its paws stick out as it walks. It's the red square that's doing all the collision detection.

▪▪ GAME DESIGN

Collision detection

Collision detection—knowing when and how two objects are touching—is a big programming challenge when building games. This book uses simple collision detection in most games, but Dog's Dinner uses a collision-detection sprite.

▽ Simple collision detection
This method simply checks whether the player sprite is touching a hazard. It's fine for simple games, but without extra code you don't know which part of the player is touching and how much is overlapping. And animating the sprite may mean its paws stick out when you swap costumes, creating false collisions.

BUMP!

▽ Collision-detection sprite
Using a simple rectangle with an animated sprite on top (like our red square and blue dog) avoids the problem with costumes, because the PlayerBlock is always the same shape and size. But you still don't know which part of it has been touched. Programming tricks like our reversing code can solve some of the problems.

BUMP!

▽ Bumper sprites
You can surround the player with "bumper" sprites that move with it and detect collisions in each direction. Knowing which direction you've hit something allows you to bounce off it correctly. Extra sprites and code blocks are needed for this type of detection.

BUMP to the front!

▽ Mathematical collision detection
If you know where everything in the game is and exactly what size it is, then by using clever math you can figure out when and how things hit each other. But be warned: this can get really complicated, as you can see below!

BUMP!

if sqrt((dogx−jellyx)^2+(dogy−jellyy)^2) < (dogR+jellyR) then BUMP!

Howling dog

To give your blue dog more personality, make him howl with disappointment when the game ends.

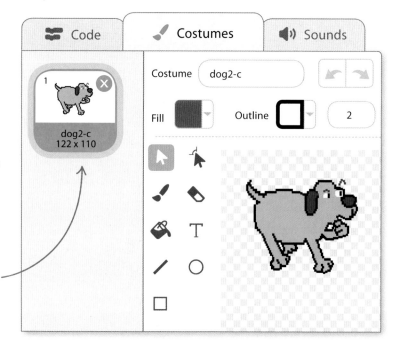

Costume dog2-c

Fill   Outline   2

dog2-c
122 x 110

29 Load the Dog2 sprite from the library again as a new sprite, but keep only the dog2-c costume this time. Rename the sprite "Howling Dog". Load the "Wolf Howl" sound from the sound library.

Delete the dog2-a and dog2-b costumes, because you need only dog2-c.

30 Add these two code blocks to make Howling Dog appear when the game ends.

The Howling Dog sprite is hidden until the message "GameOver" is broadcast.

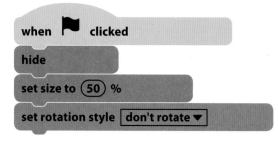

```
when ⚑ clicked
hide
set size to (50) %
set rotation style [don't rotate ▼]
```

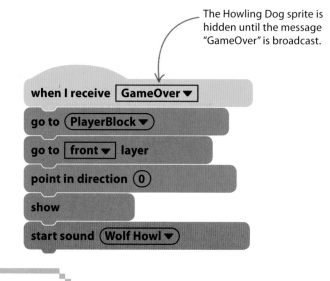

```
when I receive [GameOver ▼]
go to (PlayerBlock ▼)
go to [front ▼] layer
point in direction (0)
show
start sound (Wolf Howl ▼)
```

31 Add the short code below to the original Dog2 sprite (not the new Howling Dog sprite) to make it vanish when Howling Dog appears. Run the project and see what happens when the dog falls off the platform.

Here we go again!

```
when I receive [GameOver ▼]
hide
```

Making the levels

The next step is to create the game's three levels. You'll need to draw the platforms for each level by hand, matching the pictures on the next three pages as closely as you can. (You'll add the sprites later.) Skip forward to page 148 to find out how to paint the platforms—you can refer back to pages 145–7 once you've started.

▽ **Level 1**

Simple colored steps allow the dog to hop downhill, collecting bones. Watch out for the donut, which slides left and right—you need to choose just the right moment to drop past it.

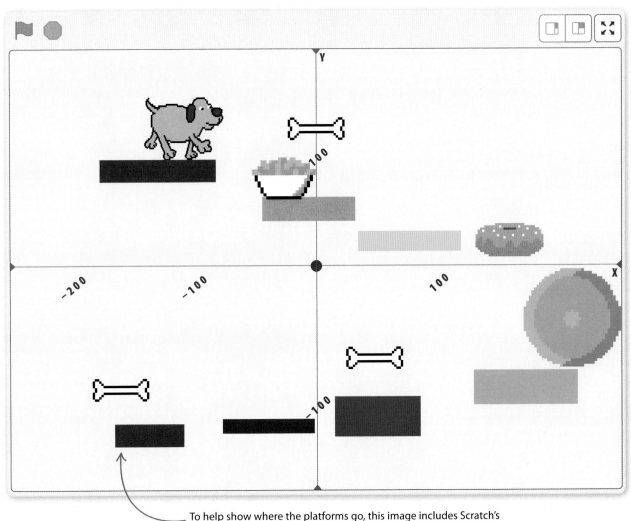

To help show where the platforms go, this image includes Scratch's xy-grid. To see the grid when you draw the platforms, select the stage info area in the lower right and click on the backdrop symbol 🖼 to open the backdrop library. Scroll to the end and choose "Xy-grid". It isn't essential to do this, but you might find it handy. You can replace the xy-grid with color backgrounds after you've made the platforms.

▽ Level 2

On Level 2, the platforms are arranged like the rungs of a ladder. You need to position the platforms very carefully so the dog can drop down without getting stuck but without making it too easy.

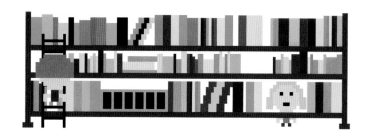

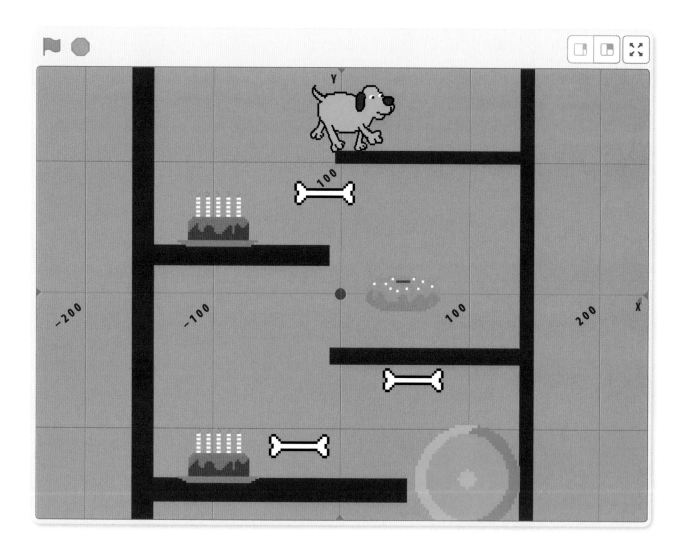

▽ **Level 3**

On the last level, some players will be tempted to try to jump over the donut, but it's a trap! It's much easier to collect the first bone and then go back left to avoid the donut altogether.

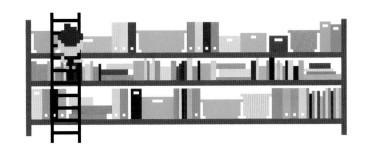

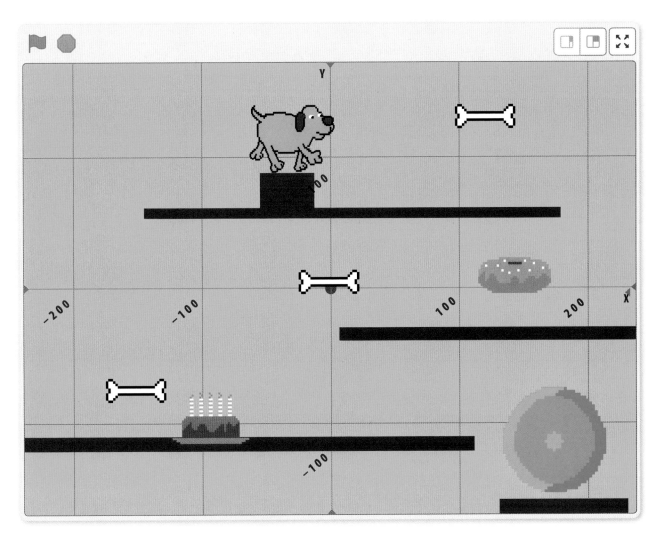

Drawing the platforms

Now to create the platforms. Dog's Dinner has three levels, so you need to create three sets of platforms. Each one will be a costume in the Platforms sprite.

32 Create a variable called "Level" for the game's three levels. Uncheck the box so that it doesn't show on the stage. To make the game use the correct level costume, add this code to the Platforms sprite. Before you start drawing, click once on this code with the mouse. This runs just this code, centering the sprite on the stage so that platforms will appear in the correct position when you draw them.

Create a new message called "Setup", which we'll use later to reset the game each time it starts.

This block changes the colored backgrounds.

```
when I receive  Setup ▼
switch backdrop to           Level
go to x: (0) y: (0)
switch costume to           Level
```

This block changes the platforms.

33 With the Platforms sprite selected, click on the Costumes tab and then use the paintbrush symbol in the costumes menu to create three new costumes. Delete the old test platform costume. Then use the rectangle tool to draw the platforms on each level. Try to match the pictures on the previous pages. Don't worry about getting them perfect; as you can adjust them later.

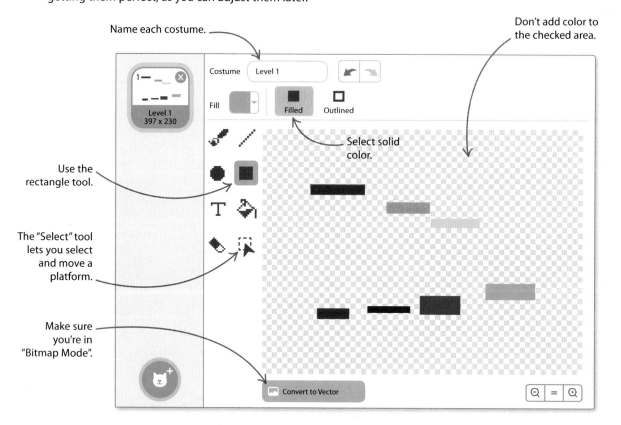

Name each costume.

Don't add color to the checked area.

Select solid color.

Use the rectangle tool.

The "Select" tool lets you select and move a platform.

Make sure you're in "Bitmap Mode".

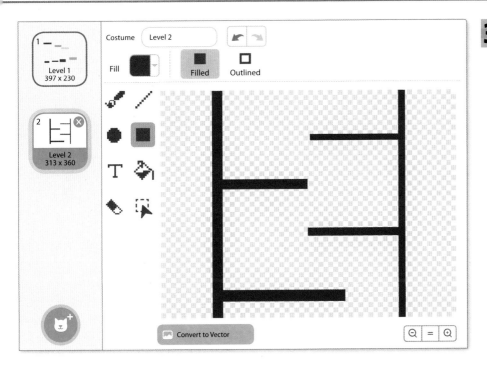

Make sure the costumes appear in the correct order here. You can drag and drop them to change the order.

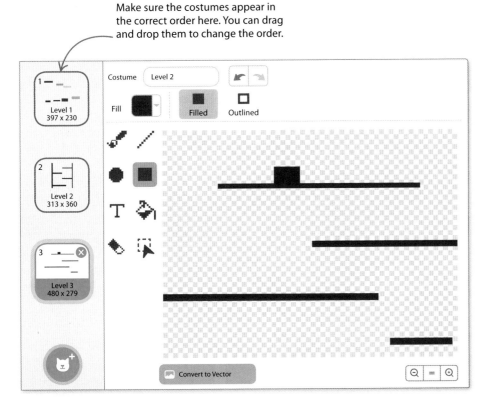

34 To add color to the backgrounds, select the stage info area to the right of the sprites list and then the Backdrops tab. Select "Convert to Bitmap" and use the fill tool to fill the paint area with color. Delete the "XY-grid", then click on the paintbrush symbol in the backdrops menu to make a new backdrop and fill it with a different color. Repeat to make a third backdrop.

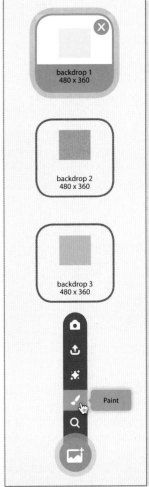

Creating a game control sprite

To make the levels change and set the start positions of all the objects on each level, you will need to build some control code. It's a good idea to keep this code in its own sprite.

I have you under my complete control!

You have me under your complete control!

35 Create two variables, "Bones" (to count the number of bones left on the level) and "LevelOver" (to show when the player has finished the current level). Uncheck their boxes. Make an empty sprite using the paintbrush symbol in the sprites menu. Name it "Game Control". Add the following code. It's a loop that repeats for every level. You also need to make two new messages: "Start" and "Win".

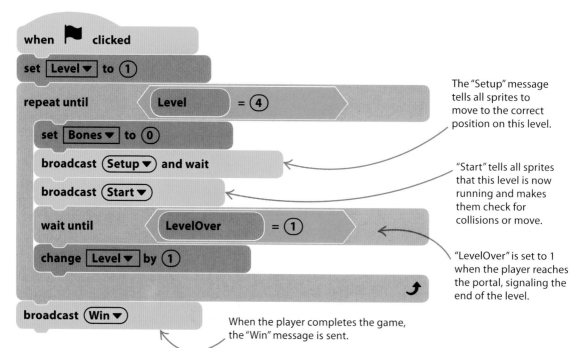

The "Setup" message tells all sprites to move to the correct position on this level.

"Start" tells all sprites that this level is now running and makes them check for collisions or move.

"LevelOver" is set to 1 when the player reaches the portal, signaling the end of the level.

When the player completes the game, the "Win" message is sent.

△ **How it works**

This code goes once around the loop for each level of the game. Then it moves on to the next block, which broadcasts a "Win" message to say that the player has won. The first broadcast is the message "Setup", which gets the sprites and background in position ready for the start of this level. It waits for all the receiving blocks to finish setting up before moving on. Then the "Start" message is sent. This triggers all the working code blocks for the level, which move the sprites and look out for collisions.

That's what happens when you go looking for collisions!

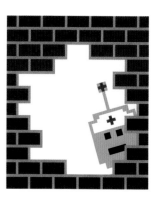

36 Change the PlayerBlock's main code so that the Game Control sprite's loop can trigger it with the "Start" message.

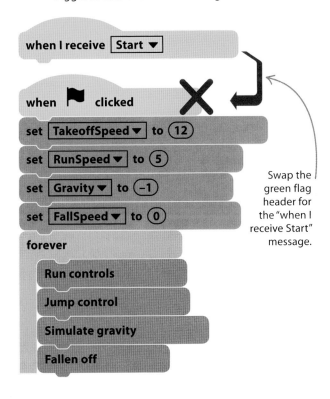

```
when I receive Start ▼

when ⚑ clicked    ✗
set TakeoffSpeed ▼ to 12
set RunSpeed ▼ to 5
set Gravity ▼ to -1
set FallSpeed ▼ to 0
forever
    Run controls
    Jump control
    Simulate gravity
    Fallen off
```

Swap the green flag header for the "when I receive Start" message.

37 With the PlayerBlock sprite still selected, add this next bit of code to set its start position for each level when the "Setup" message is received. The code starts by ghosting the sprite completely, so that you see only the dog, not the red square. Ghosting is different from hiding a sprite because collisions can still occur—which is exactly what we want!

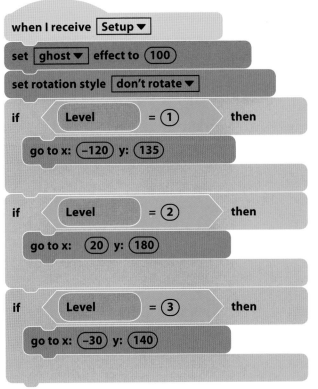

```
when I receive Setup ▼
set ghost ▼ effect to 100
set rotation style don't rotate ▼
if  Level = 1  then
    go to x: -120 y: 135

if  Level = 2  then
    go to x: 20 y: 180

if  Level = 3  then
    go to x: -30 y: 140
```

38 You also need to change Dog2's code so that it's triggered by the "Start" message.

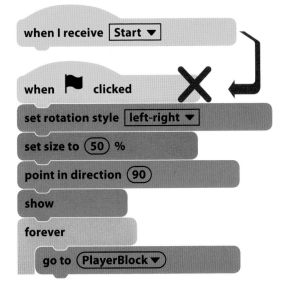

```
when I receive Start ▼

when ⚑ clicked    ✗
set rotation style left-right ▼
set size to 50 %
point in direction 90
show
forever
    go to PlayerBlock ▼
```

Placing the portals

Your game needs portals for the player to be able to progress through the levels. A portal is like a doorway that opens up when the player has completed a level.

> Is this the portal to the next level?

> No. It's the door to the next room!

39 Try running the project again. You should be able to run and jump on the Level 1 platforms, but at the moment there's no way to get to Level 2. Click the sprite symbol 🐱 in the sprites list to open the sprites library. Add Button1 to your game and change its name to "Portal".

40 The portal needs some "Setup" code to position it correctly in each level and to make it slightly see-through before it opens.

"LevelOver" is set to 0 to show that the level is not over because the bones haven't been collected.

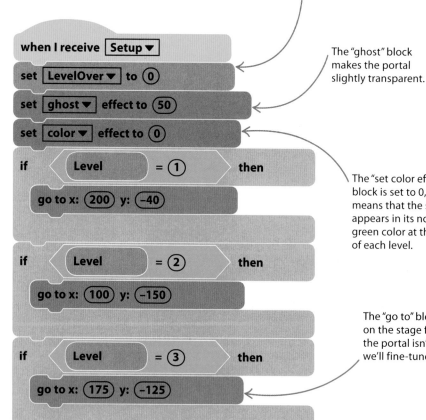

```
when I receive  Setup ▼
set  LevelOver ▼  to (0)
set  ghost ▼  effect to (50)
set  color ▼  effect to (0)
if <  Level  = (1) > then
    go to x: (200) y: (-40)
if <  Level  = (2) > then
    go to x: (100) y: (-150)
if <  Level  = (3) > then
    go to x: (175) y: (-125)
```

The "ghost" block makes the portal slightly transparent.

The "set color effect to" block is set to 0, which means that the sprite appears in its normal green color at the start of each level.

> Bones?? I'd rather have some fish!

The "go to" blocks set the portal's position on the stage for each level. Don't worry if the portal isn't in quite the right place—we'll fine-tune everything later.

41 The portal's second block of code waits for the bones to be collected and opens the portal by showing it changing color until the player touches it. Run the game. We haven't added bones to the game yet, so the portal will open immediately. You should be able to run through all the levels. If you can't, go back and carefully check all the steps.

The open portal is no longer ghosted.

Setting "LevelOver" to 1 triggers a change of level.

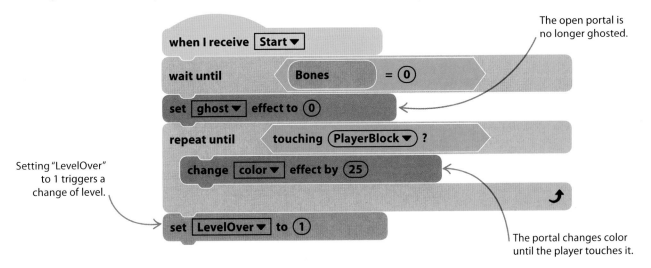

The portal changes color until the player touches it.

⬛ ⬛ ⬛ **LINGO**

Flags

"LevelOver" is a variable that the portal's code uses to tell the Game Control sprite when the level is complete. (Remember the "wait until" block in the Game Control sprite's loop? It makes the code wait before switching to the new level.) "LevelOver" allows different parts of a program to communicate. Programmers call a variable used in this way a "flag", and it is an alternative to using a message.

Flag unset
LevelOver = 0

When "LevelOver" is 0 (because the level isn't over), we say that the flag is unset. When "LevelOver" is 1 (because the player has reached the open portal), we say that the flag is set. Messages can only start code blocks, but by using a flag you can pause the code in the middle until something happens. In the Game Control sprite's loop, the "wait until" block pauses until the flag equals 1.

Flag set
LevelOver = 1

Bones for the dog

It's not much fun just racing through the levels without having anything else to do. Let's add some bones that the dog must collect to open the portal. After all, he's getting hungry!

42 Create a new sprite and draw a bone about the same size as the dog. Use the paintbrush tool for the black outline and the fill tool to color it white. Call it "Bone1". Make sure you are in bitmap mode.

Bone1

BONE 1

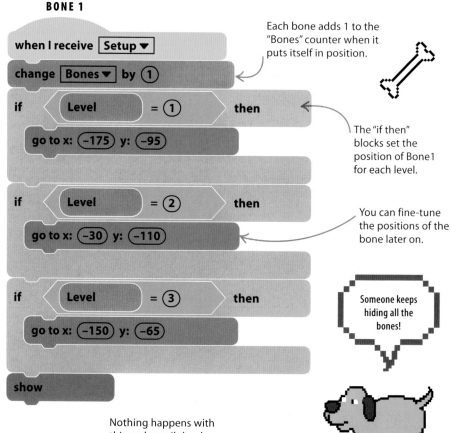

43 Add the code on the right to set Bone1's position on each level. The x and y coordinates determine where this bone will appear on the stage at each level of the game. The positions may not match your platform designs exactly, but they'll be fine for now.

```
when I receive [Setup ▼]
change [Bones ▼] by (1)
if < [Level] = (1) > then
    go to x: (-175) y: (-95)
if < [Level] = (2) > then
    go to x: (-30) y: (-110)
if < [Level] = (3) > then
    go to x: (-150) y: (-65)
show
```

Each bone adds 1 to the "Bones" counter when it puts itself in position.

The "if then" blocks set the position of Bone1 for each level.

You can fine-tune the positions of the bone later on.

Someone keeps hiding all the bones!

Nothing happens with this code until the dog touches the bone.

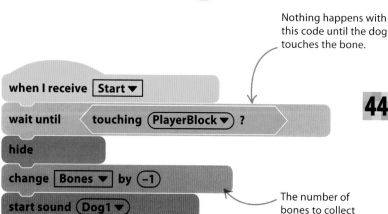

```
when I receive [Start ▼]
wait until < touching (PlayerBlock ▼) ? >
hide
change [Bones ▼] by (-1)
start sound (Dog1 ▼)
```

The number of bones to collect falls by 1.

44 Add the "Start" code shown on the left to Bone1 to make it hide when the dog collects it. It also updates the "Bones" counter. Load the sound "Dog1" to this sprite, so the dog gives a happy "woof" when he gets a bone. Run the project. At the moment, you should only have to collect one bone before the portal opens.

45 The game needs more than one bone, so right-click on the Bone1 sprite and select "duplicate". Do this twice. This will give you three bone sprites.

That's more like it!

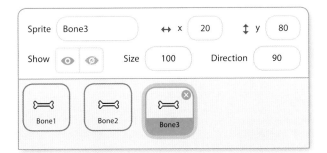

46 You need to change the "Setup" code blocks for Bone2 and Bone3 so that they appear in different places from Bone1 on each level. Change the numbers in the "go to" blocks to match those shown here.

BONE 3

when I receive Setup ▼

change Bones ▼ by (1)

if < Level = (1) > then

  go to x: (35) y: (-70)

if < Level = (2) > then

  go to x: (60) y: (-60)

if < Level = (3) > then

  go to x: (120) y: (140)

show

BONE 2

when I receive Setup ▼

change Bones ▼ by (1)

if < Level = (1) > then

  go to x: (-10) y: (105)

if < Level = (2) > then

  go to x: (-10) y: (80)

if < Level = (3) > then

  go to x: (0) y: (15)

show

These blocks test which level the bone is on and set its position on the stage.

47 The bones' code blocks manage the number of bones on a level automatically. Run the project. You should find that the portal won't open until you've collected all three bones.

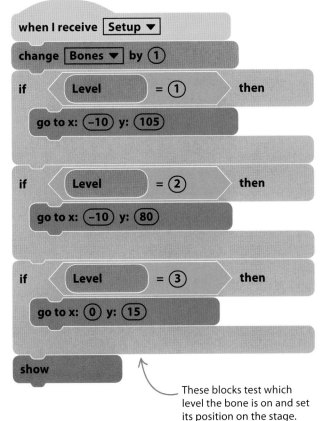

Junk food

The dog is having a rather easy time of it with all those bones to eat. Adding some obstacles and hazards will make the game more difficult. Start with the flying donut.

48 Go to the sprites library and select "Donut" to load it into the game.

Load this donut sprite.

49 Now add this "Setup" code to shrink and position the donut for each level.

This sets the donut at the correct size.

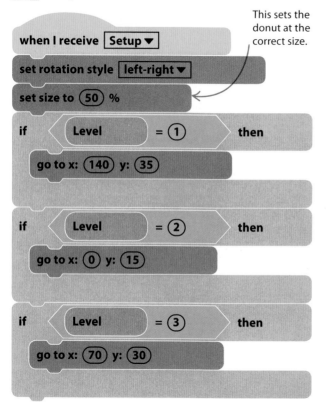

50 Next, add this "Start" code to get the donut patrolling back and forth.

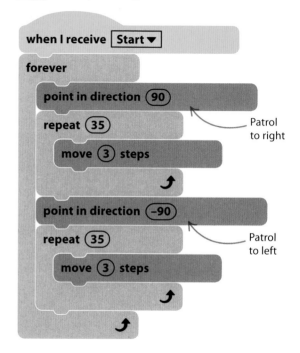

Patrol to right

Patrol to left

51 Add one last bit of code to detect a collision with the PlayerBlock and end the game—junk food really is bad for you!

52 Now run the game and try getting past the donut. If you hit the donut, the dog will stop and howl.

ARRRRGH! JUNK FOOD!

Hazardous snacks

As well as the flying donuts there are a number of fixed traps on the levels. To keep things simple, all these hazards are part of a single sprite with three different costumes—one for each level.

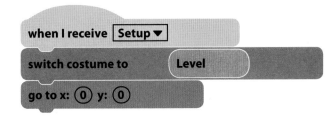

This code ends the game if the dog touches a hazard.

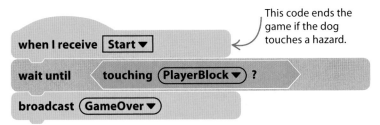

53 Create a new blank sprite called "Hazards" and add the two code blocks shown here. The "Setup" code selects the correct costume for the level and centers it on the stage (just like in Platforms). Click on the "Setup" code to center the sprite before you design its costumes.

54 You need three costumes for the Hazards sprite. Click on "Choose a Costume" at the lower left of the window and select "Cheesy Puffs" as the first costume. Click on this button twice more to add two "Cake-a" sprites as the second and third costumes. Delete "costume1" from the costumes list. Use the Select tool to make all the costumes smaller and position them as shown here. You can fine-tune their positions later.

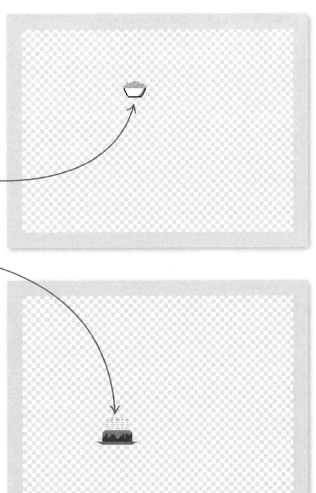

Use a bowl of cheese puffs in Level 1.

Most of the costume should have the checked pattern for a see-through color.

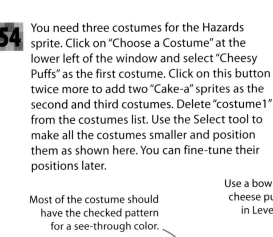

Use two cakes in Level 2.

Use one cake in Level 3.

Fine-tuning

Now that your platforms, portals, bones, and hazards are all in roughly the right place, run the project and see if the game works. You might find that some sprites aren't positioned correctly. The game might be too tricky or the dog might get stuck. If so, you need to fine-tune your levels. The hints and tips here will also be handy if you want to design new levels.

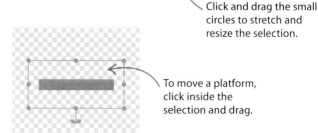

Click and drag the small circles to stretch and resize the selection.

55 Most problems can be fixed by adjusting the positions and sizes of the platforms. Select the Platforms sprite and click the Costumes tab. Use the "Select" tool in the paint editor to move, stretch, or resize the Level 1 platforms. Click outside the selection box to show your changes on the stage. Adjust the platforms until Level 1 matches page 145.

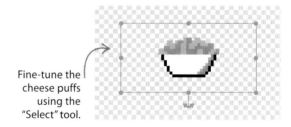

To move a platform, click inside the selection and drag.

56 Use the same method to fine-tune the position of the Hazards sprite. Select it in the sprites list and click on the Costumes tab. Use the "Select" tool to adjust the position of the snack in the first costume (which appears in Level 1). Click outside the selection box to check your changes on the stage.

Fine-tune the cheese puffs using the "Select" tool.

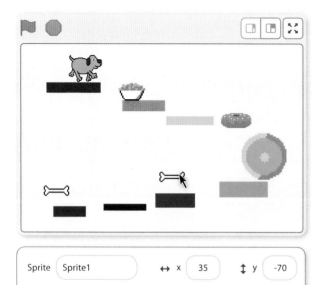

57 You can reposition all the other sprites by using their x and y coordinates. Select a sprite on the stage and drag it where you want. Make a note of its x and y numbers that appear in the information panel. Copy the numbers into the blue "go to" block in the sprite's Level 1 code.

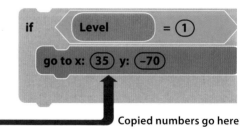

Copied numbers go here

EXPERT TIPS

The "go to" trick

To reposition a sprite perfectly, use this sneaky trick. First drag the sprite on the stage to where you want it. Then look at the unused "go to" block in the Motion section under the Code tab. The sprite's coordinates will have appeared automatically in this block. Now you can simply drag the block into your code without needing to do any typing. Easy!

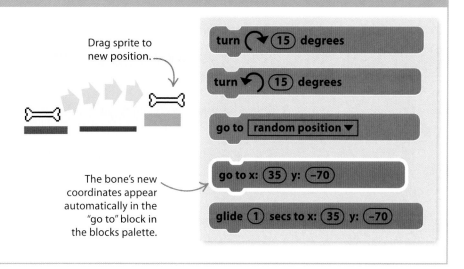

Drag sprite to new position.

The bone's new coordinates appear automatically in the "go to" block in the blocks palette.

turn ↻ (15) degrees

turn ↺ (15) degrees

go to [random position ▼]

go to x: (35) y: (−70)

glide (1) secs to x: (35) y: (−70)

58 If you need to move the sliding donut, bear in mind that the "go to" block sets its start position. To change how far it slides, adjust the numbers in its two "repeat" loops. One controls how far it goes to the right, the other to the left.

59 You should now have Level 1 working beautifully. To work on another level and its sprites, you can make a temporary change to the code for the Game Control sprite. Change the number in the "set Level to" block to "2". Run the game and Level 2 appears on the stage. Fine-tune your sprites' positions. But remember to change the number in "set Level to" back to "1" when you're done.

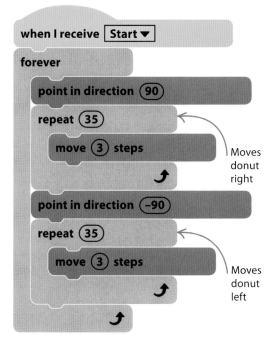

when I receive [Start ▼]

forever

  point in direction (90)

  repeat (35)

    move (3) steps

Moves donut right

  point in direction (−90)

  repeat (35)

    move (3) steps

Moves donut left

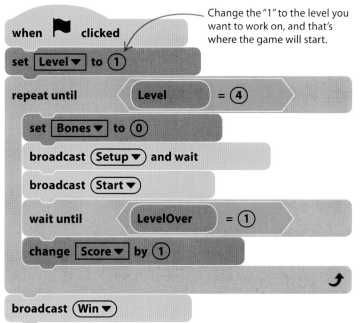

Change the "1" to the level you want to work on, and that's where the game will start.

when ⚑ clicked

set [Level ▼] to (1)

repeat until ⟨ Level = (4) ⟩

  set [Bones ▼] to (0)

  broadcast (Setup ▼) and wait

  broadcast (Start ▼)

  wait until ⟨ LevelOver = (1) ⟩

  change [Score ▼] by (1)

broadcast (Win ▼)

Signs and music

The game won't be complete until you've added some instructions and other messages for the player. You can also load some music into it to make it even more entertaining.

60 To give instructions and other messages to the player, use the paintbrush symbol in the sprites menu to create a new blank sprite and call it "Signs". Then use the paintbrush symbol in the costumes menu to add the costumes below to the Signs sprite. Name them "Instructions", "Win", and "Lose".

Instructions

```
DOG'S DINNER                   MOVE: ARROW KEYS
                               JUMP: SPACE BAR




COLLECT ALL BONES              DOG DOES NOT LIKE
TO OPEN PORTAL TO              JUNK FOOD!
NEXT LEVEL
```

61 To show the correct sign to the player when the Signs sprite receives a message, add the three code blocks below. Run the project to check that the correct signs show as you play.

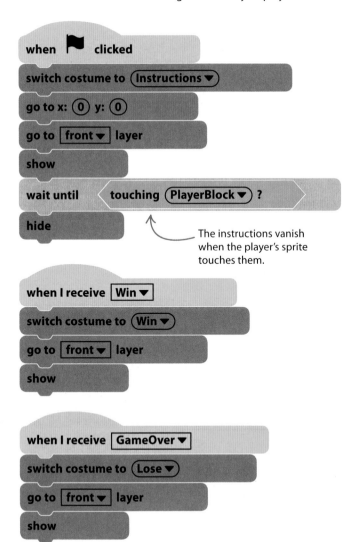

The instructions vanish when the player's sprite touches them.

Win

```
YOU WIN!
```

Lose

```
ARRRRGH!
JUNK FOOD!
```

62 Check the positions of the instructions. You may need to rearrange them so that they don't overlap the images on the stage.

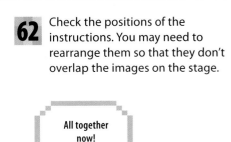

All together now!

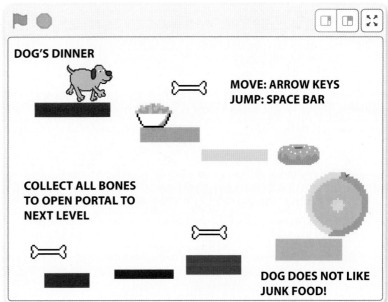

DOG'S DINNER

MOVE: ARROW KEYS
JUMP: SPACE BAR

COLLECT ALL BONES
TO OPEN PORTAL TO
NEXT LEVEL

DOG DOES NOT LIKE
JUNK FOOD!

63 You can give each level its own music. Select the Game Control sprite and load these sounds from the Scratch sound library: "Xylo2", "Xylo3", and "Xylo4". The code below will swap the music each time you change levels.

64 Add the next bit of code to the Game Control sprite to swap the music at the moment the new level starts and to announce the start of each level with a sound effect. Load the "Space Ripple" sound into the sprite.

The first "repeat" loop plays "Xylo2" until the player reaches Level 2.

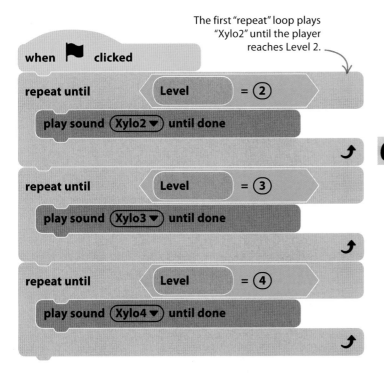

```
when [flag] clicked
repeat until   Level  = (2)
    play sound (Xylo2 ▼) until done

repeat until   Level  = (3)
    play sound (Xylo3 ▼) until done

repeat until   Level  = (4)
    play sound (Xylo4 ▼) until done
```

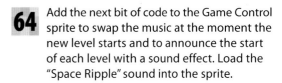

```
when I receive [Start ▼]
stop all sounds
start sound (Space Ripple ▼)
```

65 To play a victory tune when the dog finishes the final level, load "Triumph" from the sound library and add this code to the Game Control sprite. Run the game. Check that the music changes for each level, and that sound effects play at the start of each level and at the end of the game.

```
when I receive [Win ▼]
stop all sounds
start sound (Triumph ▼)
```

Hacks and tweaks

Congratulations, your platform game is up and running! Test it and ask your friends to play it. You may need to adjust the sprites' positions and edit your platforms and hazards a little to make the game play smoothly and to get the difficulty level just right.

▽ **Victory dance**

If you think the end of the game isn't exciting enough, change the code for the "Win" message to do something more spectacular. Maybe the dog could do a little victory dance? Why not add a new sign for when the dog falls off the platforms and ends up at the bottom of the stage? You could make the dog disappear too.

EXPERT TIPS
Backing up

Save a backup copy of the game under a different name before you start making changes. If you do this, you'll always have the copy to go back to if you make mistakes when tweaking the code. To save with the online Scratch editor, select the File menu and click on "Save as a copy".

> You won!
> Let's celebrate!

> Oh, it was nothing really!

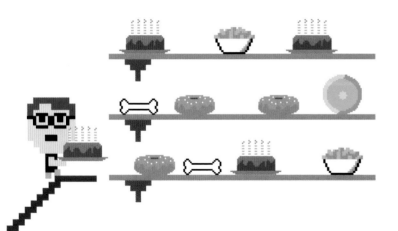

◁ **Extra levels**

To make the game longer you could create extra levels. You would have to give the Platforms and Hazards sprites more costumes, and edit the code blocks to add "if Level =" blocks to place the bones, portal, and donut at the start of each level. Don't forget to change the "Level = 4" block in the Game Control sprite's loop, so that the game will end after the player has completed all the new levels.

▷ **Mega-challenge**

Can you figure out how to give the dog a limited number of lives? You'd need a new variable called "Lives", and you'd have to reprogram all the "GameOver" messages to subtract 1 from the variable until you reach the last life. The Game Control sprite's loop would also need changing. It's an expert programming challenge that needs clear thinking and hard work!

Increasing this number makes the dog jump higher.

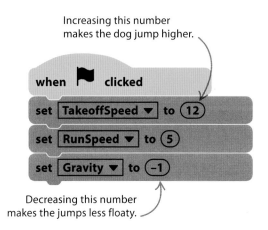

Decreasing this number makes the jumps less floaty.

◁ **Adjust the jump**

You have total control over the dog's jumps. You can make him leap higher by increasing the value of the "TakeoffSpeed" variable. You can also make the value of "Gravity" smaller or larger to control how much each jump floats. Why not add a special level with reverse gravity, so that gravity pulls you up, not down? You will need to make code changes to set the jump variables just for that level with an "if then" block, and also to detect when the dog "falls" off the top of the level!

GAME DESIGN

Designing levels

Designing how all the challenges and rewards in a level fit together is a tricky job. You need to plan every detail and get a friend to test it to see if it's too easy or too hard. Make sure you can complete the level yourself before asking the friend to try.

Timing Are your moving hazards going so fast you can't get past them, or so slow there's no challenge? Adjust their speeds until you're happy with them.

Spacing Is the player able to jump from platform to platform easily—or perhaps too easily? Make the gaps between the platforms bigger or smaller to suit the level you're designing.

Tricks Try fooling the player into following what appears to be an obvious way through a level but then turns out to be a trap. The correct way will be an easier, but less obvious solution.

Tools Computer games often come with level design tools that are unlocked once you finish the game. Using these you can create your own challenges and puzzles within the game. You can usually share your customized levels online so that others can try them.

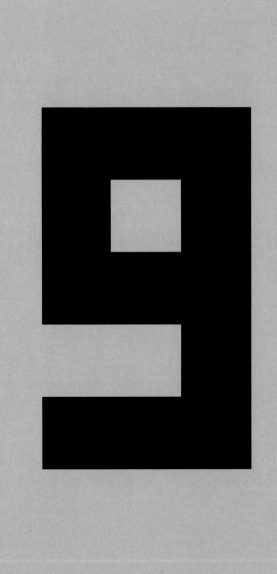

Glacier Race

How to build Glacier Race

Glacier Race is a two-player game in which you race up the screen, swerving around obstacles and collecting gems as you go. There's no finish line in this race—the winner is simply the person with the most gems when the time runs out.

AIM OF THE GAME

It's red car versus blue car in a race against the clock. Win by collecting more gems than your opponent before the countdown ends. Every gem you grab adds an extra second to the race countdown, but stay clear of the snow, or you'll end up in a spin.

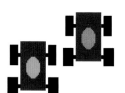

◁ **Cars**
Use the game controls to keep your car on the ice and collect gems. You can also push the other car off the road to gain an advantage.

◁ **Obstacles**
Avoid the giant snowballs and the edge of the road, or you'll spin out of control.

◁ **Penguin**
The penguin is the master of ceremonies. He asks the players' names at the start, gives instructions, and announces the winner at the end.

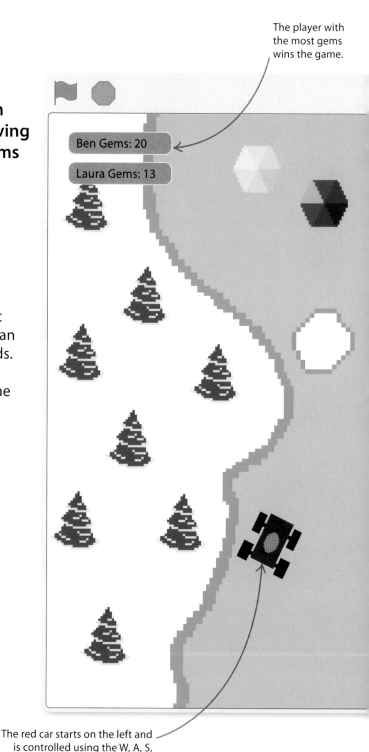

The player with the most gems wins the game.

Ben Gems: 20

Laura Gems: 13

The red car starts on the left and is controlled using the W, A, S, and D keys on the keyboard.

Collect gems to score a point and add a second to the countdown so you can race a little longer.

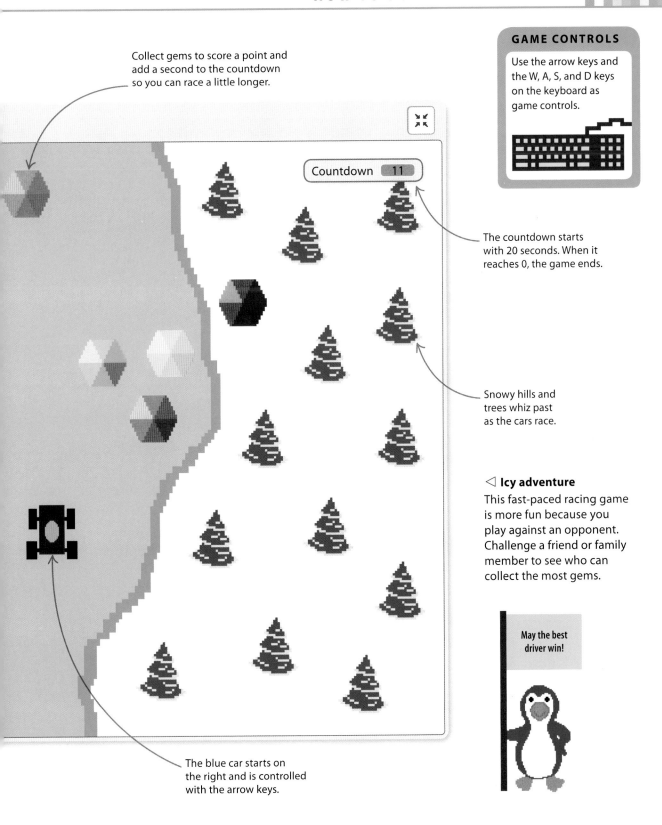

Countdown 11

The countdown starts with 20 seconds. When it reaches 0, the game ends.

Snowy hills and trees whiz past as the cars race.

The blue car starts on the right and is controlled with the arrow keys.

GAME CONTROLS

Use the arrow keys and the W, A, S, and D keys on the keyboard as game controls.

◁ **Icy adventure**
This fast-paced racing game is more fun because you play against an opponent. Challenge a friend or family member to see who can collect the most gems.

May the best driver win!

The game loop

Fast games need clever code. This game uses something called a "game loop" to keep all the action happening just when it should. It's as if the game loop bangs a drum, and with each beat, all the other sprites move one step. Start by creating a blank sprite to hold the game loop's code.

1 Start a new project and delete the cat sprite. Use the paintbrush symbol ✎ to create a blank sprite and rename it "Game Loop". Then make a variable called "Countdown" for the game timer and show it on the stage. Build the following code to make the game loop. You'll need to create the messages "Setup", "Calculate", "Move", and "GameOver".

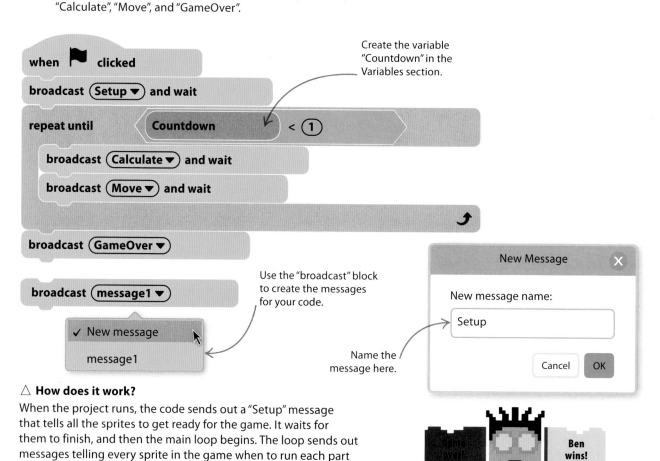

Create the variable "Countdown" in the Variables section.

```
when 🏴 clicked

broadcast (Setup ▼) and wait

repeat until ⟨ Countdown ⟩ < 1

    broadcast (Calculate ▼) and wait

    broadcast (Move ▼) and wait

broadcast (GameOver ▼)

broadcast (message1 ▼)
    ✓ New message
      message1
```

Use the "broadcast" block to create the messages for your code.

New Message ✕

New message name:

Setup

Cancel   OK

Name the message here.

△ **How does it work?**

When the project runs, the code sends out a "Setup" message that tells all the sprites to get ready for the game. It waits for them to finish, and then the main loop begins. The loop sends out messages telling every sprite in the game when to run each part of their code. The loop ends only when the countdown reaches 0, at which point the "GameOver" message is sent so all sprites can perform any final actions and the winner is announced.

Game over!   Ben wins!

Game loops

Using one main loop to keep everything in sync is common in computer games. The loop keeps all the sprites in step and makes the code tidy and short. It also helps the game run quickly—in Glacier Race, the game loop runs as fast as 30 times per second. In Scratch, a program with lots of sprites each with its own loops can become slow as the computer has to constantly jump between them. Using a single game loop fixes this problem, but be careful not to use loops elsewhere in the game because they will slow it down.

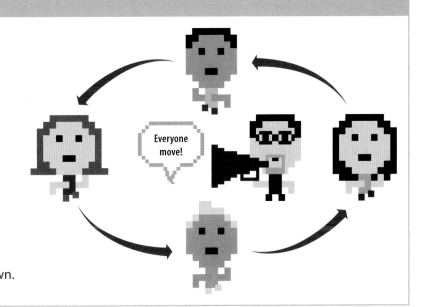

Everyone move!

2 Create two new variables: "RoadY" (to store the y coordinate used to position our moving scenery) and "CarSpeed" (to set how quickly the cars can move around the stage). Uncheck the boxes in the Variables section so they aren't displayed on the stage. Add the code on the right to set the values of the variables at the start of the game.

```
when I receive  Setup ▼
set  RoadY ▼  to  0
set  CarSpeed ▼  to  5
set  Countdown ▼  to  20
reset timer
```

This block sets the time limit for the game in seconds.

3 Add another variable for all sprites called "RoadSpeed" to store the speed of the moving scenery. Uncheck the box. Then create a code to calculate the position of the road each time the game loop runs. You'll see how this works once you've made the road sprites.

The y coordinate of the road decreases from 360 to –360 before jumping back to 360 as the road repeats itself.

```
when I receive  Calculate ▼
set  RoadSpeed ▼  to  -5
change  RoadY ▼  by        RoadSpeed
if          RoadY          <  -360          then
    change  RoadY ▼  by  720
```

Scrolling road

In Glacier Race, players feel as if they're moving quickly along the road, but in reality their cars don't move very far on the stage—it's the road that moves instead. The road is made up of two sprites that fit together seamlessly: Road1 and Road2. These roads take turns scrolling down the stage, making the cars appear to move faster than they really do.

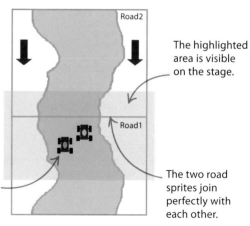

Road2

The highlighted area is visible on the stage.

The cars appear to move forward as Road1 and Road2 move down the stage.

Road1

The two road sprites join perfectly with each other.

4 Create a new sprite and call it "Road1". In the paint editor, choose the paintbrush tool ✏ and set the thickness to 10. Draw the edges of the road, and make sure they run all the way from the top to the bottom without any gaps. Then use the fill tool 🪣 to color the area on both sides of the road white, creating a snowy setting.

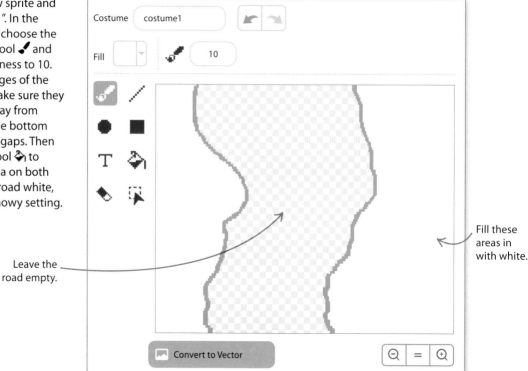

Leave the road empty.

Fill these areas in with white.

5 Now duplicate the Road1 sprite to make Road2. Select Road2 and go to the Costumes tab. Click on the "Flip vertical" button at the top right, and the road costume will turn upside down. The edges of Road1 and Road2 will now match since they are mirror images. They'll look odd on the stage at the moment, but you'll fix that later.

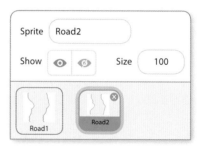

Use this tool to flip the costume upside down.

6 Add these code blocks to Road1 to get the road moving. They position the road using the "RoadY" variable in the game loop. Try running the project—half of the road will scroll down the screen.

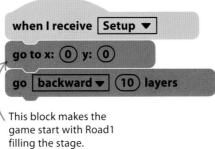

This block makes the game start with Road1 filling the stage.

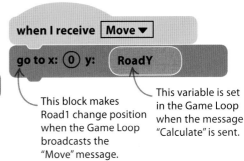

This block makes Road1 change position when the Game Loop broadcasts the "Move" message.

This variable is set in the Game Loop when the message "Calculate" is sent.

7 Now build the following code blocks for Road2 to make the second road sprite work together with the first. Run the project—the road should scroll smoothly down the screen.

This makes sure the scenery stays behind the other sprites.

Road2 is positioned above or below Road1, depending on where Road1 is on the stage.

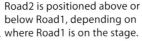

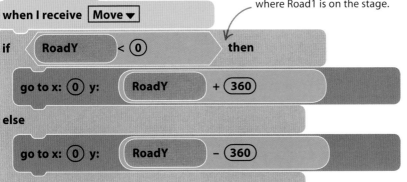

8 To add color to the road, paint the backdrop instead of the sprites, or else the cars will collide with the road surface. Select the stage, and click on the Backdrops tab. Use the fill tool 🖌 to fill it with an icy blue color.

backdrop1
480 x 360

▪▪▪ LINGO

Scrolling

Moving everything on the screen together in the same direction is called scrolling. In Glacier Race, the road scrolls downward. You might have heard of games called side-scrollers, which means the scene moves left or right as the player moves the character on the screen.

9 Make the scenery more interesting by adding some trees. Select Road1, and click on the Costumes tab. Create your own trees or bushes using the tools in the paint editor. Repeat the process for Road2.

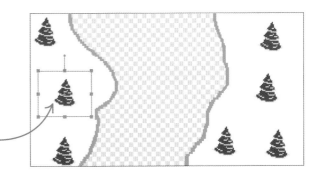

Create as many trees as you like, and place them around the road.

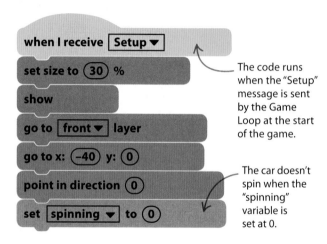

Race cars

Now it's time to add the race cars. Once you've got one car moving, you can duplicate it to make the second one and save yourself a lot of work.

10 Click the sprite symbol 🐱 and load Cat from the library—you can use this sprite to make sure the car is the right size. Now open the paint editor and click on "Convert to Bitmap". Use the rectangle and circle tools to draw a car like the one shown here. Make sure you draw the car facing right, or it will point the wrong way in the game. Remember to delete the cat image once you've finished.

Make your race car a bit bigger than the cat. The next bit of code will shrink it.

Use the circle tool to draw an oval shape.

Use the rectangle tool to draw the body and wheels of the car.

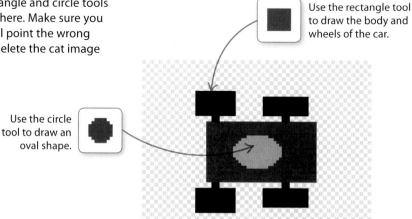

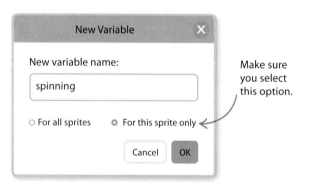

11 Rename the sprite "RedCar" in the sprites list. Then create a new variable, "spinning", which you'll use later to say when a car is in a spin. Note that for this variable, you need to select the option "for this sprite only" and uncheck the box in the Variables section so that the variable doesn't show on the stage.

New Variable   ✕

New variable name:

`spinning`

○ For all sprites   ● For this sprite only

Make sure you select this option.

Cancel   **OK**

12 Remember that in this project, sprites can run code only when they get messages from the Game Loop. Add the following code to set up the red car at the start of the game.

```
when I receive Setup ▼
set size to (30) %
show
go to front ▼ layer
go to x: (-40) y: (0)
point in direction (0)
set spinning ▼ to (0)
```

The code runs when the "Setup" message is sent by the Game Loop at the start of the game.

The car doesn't spin when the "spinning" variable is set at 0.

13 You now need to add keyboard controls for the car. Choose My Blocks in the blocks palette, and then click on "Make a Block". Create a new block called "car controls" and add this code to its "define" block.

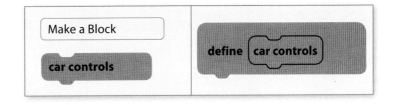

The car usually points straight up the screen.

This block moves the car sideways.

This block makes the car turn a little to the right.

This block makes the car turn a little to the left.

This block moves the car up the stage.

This block makes the car appear to stop by moving it down the stage at the same speed as the road.

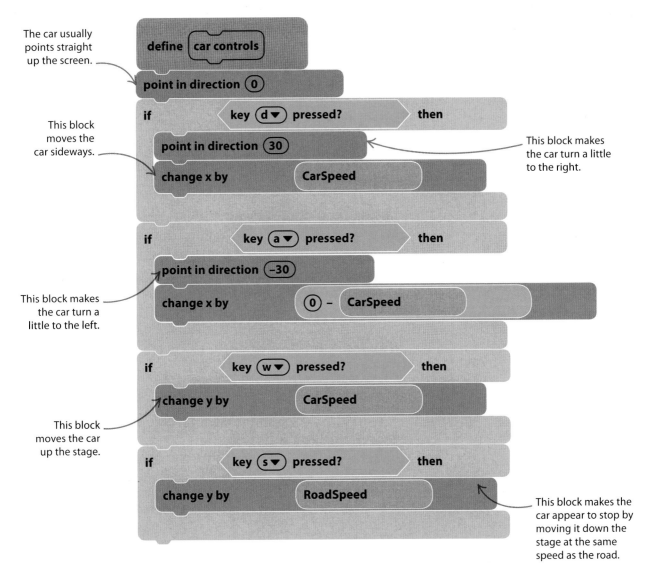

14 Add some code to run the "car controls" block when the car receives the message "Move" from the Game Loop. Run the project. You should now be able to steer the red car along the road using the keys W, A, S, and D.

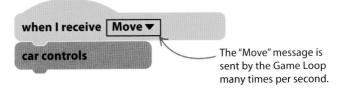

The "Move" message is sent by the Game Loop many times per second.

Collisions and spins

To make the game challenging, you can force players to avoid the snow by making their cars spin out of control if they touch it. You need to create some more new blocks to make this work.

15 With RedCar selected, create a new block to detect the snow. Choose My Blocks in the blocks palette and then click "Make a Block". Name the block "check collisions" and create the following code.

The "touching" block detects only the painted parts of the road sprite's costume, not the road itself.

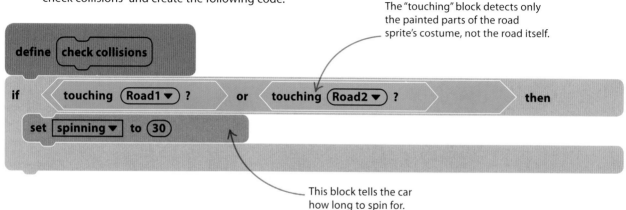

```
define check collisions

if   touching (Road1 ▼) ?   or   touching (Road2 ▼) ?   then
    set spinning ▼ to (30)
```

This block tells the car how long to spin for.

16 Now create another block, call it "spin", and add the code shown here. The "spin" block runs when the car is spinning. It turns the car around and reduces the "spinning" variable by one. When the variable reaches zero, the spin ends, and the car is reset at the bottom of the stage.

Load the sound "Rattle" from the sound library to see it in the drop-down menu.

This block moves the car down the stage as if it's stopped on the road.

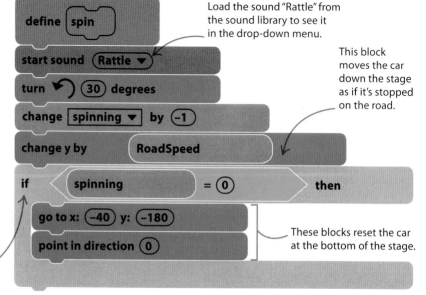

```
define spin

start sound (Rattle ▼)
turn ↻ (30) degrees
change spinning ▼ by (-1)
change y by (RoadSpeed)
if   spinning = (0)   then
    go to x: (-40) y: (-180)
    point in direction (0)
```

These blocks reset the car at the bottom of the stage.

This block checks whether the spin is over.

17 Finally, change the existing code triggered by the "Move" message to look like the one shown here. Now you can control the car only if the "spinning" variable is zero. Collisions are checked only when you're not in a spin—otherwise, you'd spin forever! Run the game. The car should spin if it hits the snow.

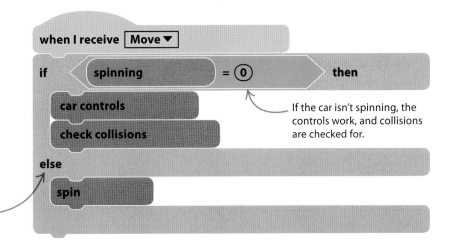

If the car isn't spinning, the controls work, and collisions are checked for.

If the value for "spinning" is more than 0, the car will spin.

18 To add some snowball obstacles, create a new sprite in the paint editor. Make it about the size of the car on the stage. To get the correct size, watch it appear on the stage after you've drawn it. You can also see the costume's size in the costume list—aim for about 40 x 40. Name the new sprite "Snowball".

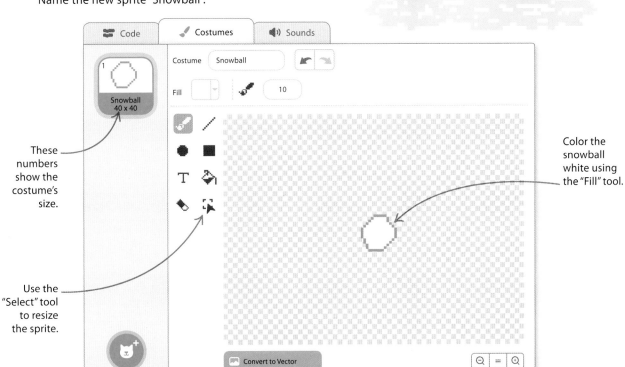

These numbers show the costume's size.

Use the "Select" tool to resize the sprite.

Color the snowball white using the "Fill" tool.

19 Add the following three code blocks to the Snowball sprite. The Snowball sprite is cloned to make lots of obstacles, but you might notice that there's no "create clone" block here. The clones will be created by the Game Loop sprite, using some code that we'll add next.

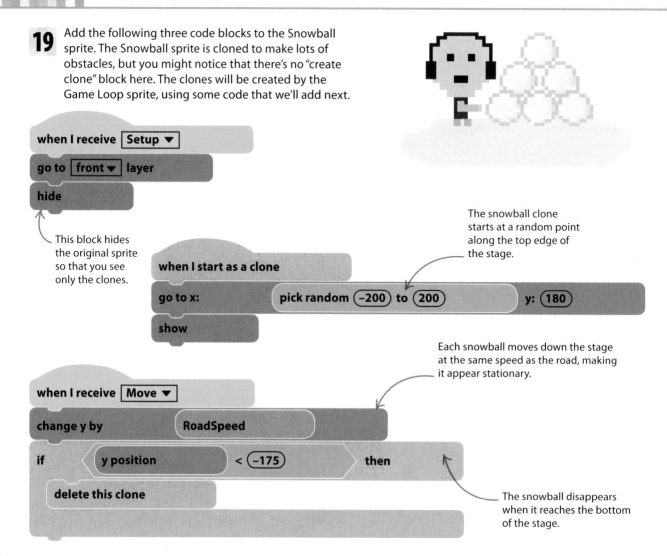

```
when I receive Setup ▼
go to front ▼ layer
hide
```

This block hides the original sprite so that you see only the clones.

The snowball clone starts at a random point along the top edge of the stage.

```
when I start as a clone
go to x: pick random (-200) to (200)   y: (180)
show
```

Each snowball moves down the stage at the same speed as the road, making it appear stationary.

```
when I receive Move ▼
change y by   RoadSpeed
if   y position   < (-175)   then
    delete this clone
```

The snowball disappears when it reaches the bottom of the stage.

20 Now select the Game Loop sprite and add this code to make a new snowball appear with a chance of 1 in 200 every time the loop repeats.

Making this number bigger creates fewer snowballs.

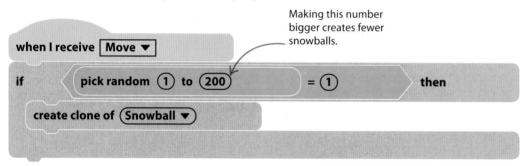

```
when I receive Move ▼
if   pick random (1) to (200)   = (1)   then
    create clone of (Snowball ▼)
```

21 To make the car spin when it hits a snowball, you need to add the Snowball sprite to the list of possible collisions for the red car. Run the game. You should now see the car spin when it hits a snowball.

Slot one "or" block into another.

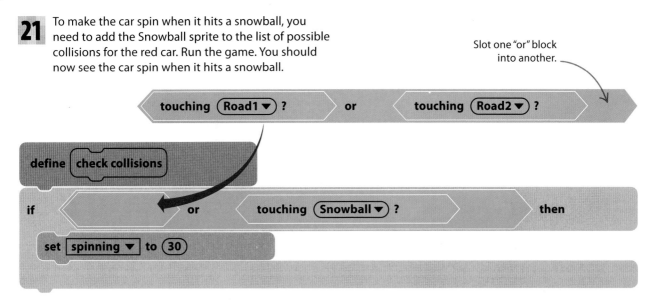

Player two

You now need to create the second player's car. Doing this is easy—you simply copy the first car, recolor it blue, and tweak the code blocks.

22 Duplicate the RedCar sprite and name the copy "BlueCar". Note that the duplicate sprite gets its own copy of all the code blocks. This includes a copy of the "spinning" variable (set to "for this sprite only"), which can be different from the red car's.

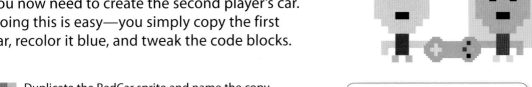

23 Select the BlueCar sprite and click on the Costumes tab to open the paint editor. Use the fill tool to change the color of the car.

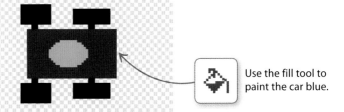

Use the fill tool to paint the car blue.

24 Now select the Code tab to see BlueCar's code. Change the x coordinates in its "go to" blocks to 40 in both the "Define spin" code and the "When I receive Setup" code. This makes the blue and red cars start next to each other.

Change the x coordinate to 40.

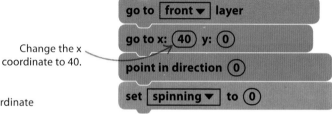

Change the x coordinate to 40 here, too.

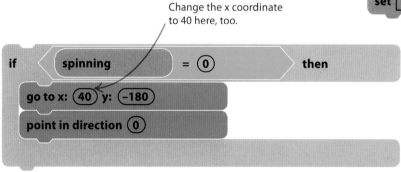

Select the arrow keys in all four "key pressed?" blocks.

25 In the "Define car controls" code, change the "key pressed" blocks so that the blue car can be steered using the arrow keys on the keyboard. Then run the game. Both the cars should race along the track, but they can drive through each other at the moment.

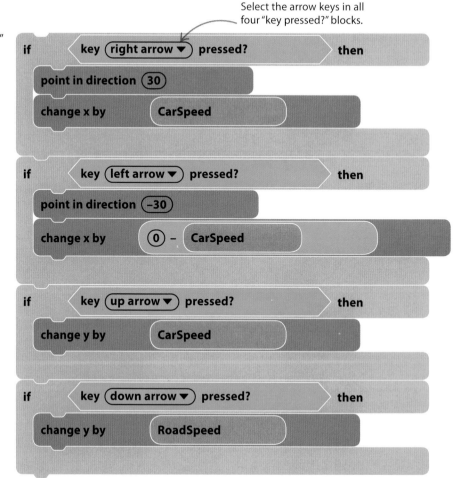

▷ **Change the code**
In the "key pressed?" blocks, replace key "d" with "right arrow", key "a" with "left arrow", key "w" with "up arrow", and key "s" with "down arrow".

26 To stop the cars from driving through each other, you need to make them sense each other and then bounce apart. Add a new "if then" block to RedCar's "Define check collisions" code as shown here. Create the message "bounce", and then add new code to make RedCar move away from BlueCar when it receives the message.

Get out of my way!

```
define check collisions

if    touching (Road1 ▼) ?    or    touching (Road2 ▼) ?    or    touching (Snowball ▼) ?    then
    set spinning ▼ to (30)

if    touching (BlueCar ▼) ?    then
    broadcast (bounce ▼)
```

Add these new blocks to the existing code.

```
when I receive bounce ▼
point towards (BlueCar ▼)
turn ↻ (180) degrees
move (20) steps
point in direction (0)
```

This new code makes RedCar bounce away from BlueCar.

27 Now make the same changes to BlueCar's code blocks so it can sense when it touches RedCar and bounce. Run the game to make sure the cars bounce when they collide.

```
if    touching (RedCar ▼) ?    then
    broadcast (bounce ▼)
```

This time the "touching" block checks for collisions with the red car.

Choose RedCar here.

```
when I receive bounce ▼
point towards (RedCar ▼)
turn ↻ (180) degrees
move (20) steps
point in direction (0)
```

Collecting gems

The next step is to create the colorful gems that the players battle to collect. Each gem will be a clone of a single gem sprite, which makes it easy to put lots of gems on the stage at once.

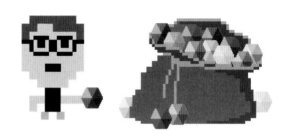

28 Click the paintbrush symbol in the sprites menu to create a new sprite with the paint editor. To create a gem, use the line tool to draw six triangles arranged in a hexagon. Fill each one with a different shade of green. Make it similar in size to the snowball.

Name the sprite "Gem".

Gem
40 x 33

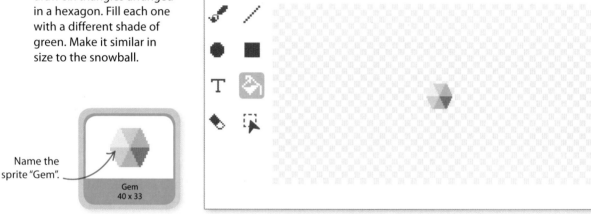

29 Create two variables—"RedCarGems" and "BlueCarGems" (both for all sprites)—to tally how many gems each car collects. Now add these code blocks to the Gem sprite; they're similar to the code blocks for the snowballs.

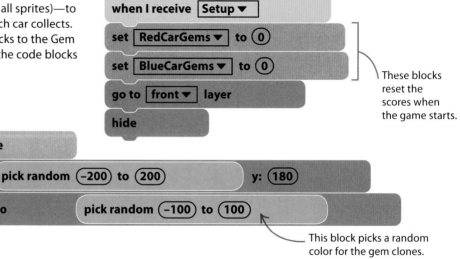

when I receive Setup ▼
set RedCarGems ▼ to 0
set BlueCarGems ▼ to 0
go to front ▼ layer
hide

These blocks reset the scores when the game starts.

when I start as a clone
go to x: pick random -200 to 200 y: 180
set color ▼ effect to pick random -100 to 100
show

This block picks a random color for the gem clones.

30 Add the following code to move the gems along with the road and to update the total number of gems collected by each car. Load the "Fairydust" sound to the Gem sprite so that it plays each time a gem is collected.

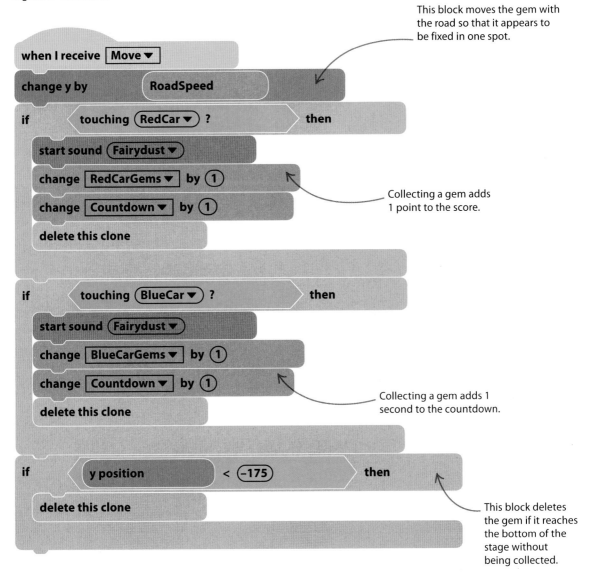

This block moves the gem with the road so that it appears to be fixed in one spot.

```
when I receive Move ▼
change y by ( RoadSpeed )
if < touching (RedCar ▼) ? > then
    start sound (Fairydust ▼)
    change [RedCarGems ▼] by (1)
    change [Countdown ▼] by (1)
    delete this clone
```

Collecting a gem adds 1 point to the score.

```
if < touching (BlueCar ▼) ? > then
    start sound (Fairydust ▼)
    change [BlueCarGems ▼] by (1)
    change [Countdown ▼] by (1)
    delete this clone
```

Collecting a gem adds 1 second to the countdown.

```
if < (y position) < (-175) > then
    delete this clone
```

This block deletes the gem if it reaches the bottom of the stage without being collected.

31 In the Game Loop sprite, add a second "if then" block to the "when I receive Move" code to create the gem clones. Run the game and try collecting gems. The snowballs will prevent players from rushing to the top and collecting all the gems. The gems and snowballs together create the balance and challenge of the game.

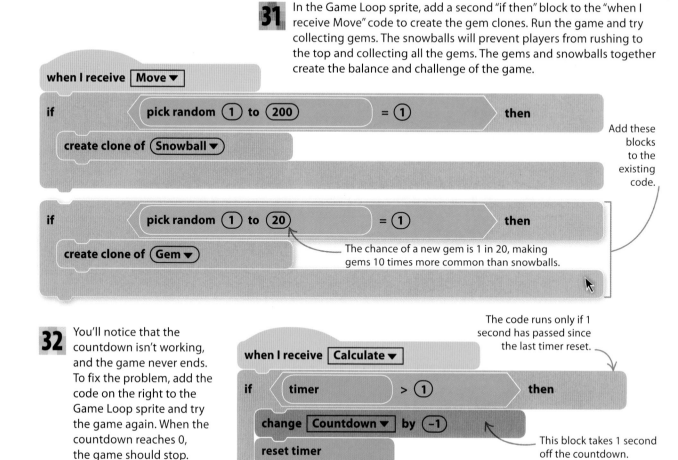

when I receive | Move ▼ |

if ⟨ pick random (1) to (200) = (1) ⟩ then

create clone of (Snowball ▼)

if ⟨ pick random (1) to (20) = (1) ⟩ then

create clone of (Gem ▼)

The chance of a new gem is 1 in 20, making gems 10 times more common than snowballs.

Add these blocks to the existing code.

32 You'll notice that the countdown isn't working, and the game never ends. To fix the problem, add the code on the right to the Game Loop sprite and try the game again. When the countdown reaches 0, the game should stop.

The code runs only if 1 second has passed since the last timer reset.

when I receive | Calculate ▼ |

if ⟨ timer > (1) ⟩ then

change | Countdown ▼ | by (-1)

reset timer

This block takes 1 second off the countdown.

if ⟨ Countdown < (10) ⟩ then

start sound (Pop ▼)

This "if then" block plays "pop" sounds in the last 10 seconds of the game to warn the players that time is running out.

Penguin in charge

A formal start and finish can make a game look more professional. Add a penguin race official to ask the players' names, start the race, and announce the winners.

33 First, create four variables for all sprites: "RedName" and "BlueName" to store each driver's name; and "RedInfo" and "BlueInfo" to show each driver's score during the race. Then add the Penguin 2 sprite to talk to the players, and load the "Gong" sound from the library to Penguin 2.

Penguin 2

34 Add this "Setup" code to the Penguin 2 sprite. The Game Loop uses a "broadcast and wait" block, so the race doesn't start until the players put in their names and the penguin shouts "Go!"

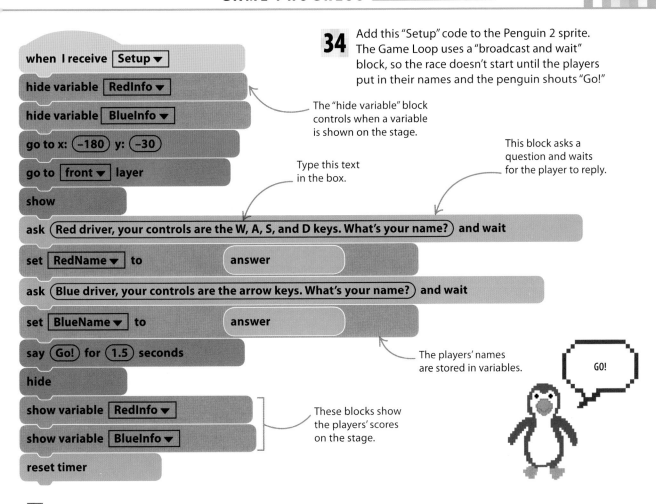

```
when I receive Setup ▼
hide variable RedInfo ▼
hide variable BlueInfo ▼
go to x: (-180) y: (-30)
go to front ▼ layer
show
ask (Red driver, your controls are the W, A, S, and D keys. What's your name?) and wait
set RedName ▼ to                     answer
ask (Blue driver, your controls are the arrow keys. What's your name?) and wait
set BlueName ▼ to                    answer
say (Go!) for (1.5) seconds
hide
show variable RedInfo ▼
show variable BlueInfo ▼
reset timer
```

The "hide variable" block controls when a variable is shown on the stage.

This block asks a question and waits for the player to reply.

Type this text in the box.

The players' names are stored in variables.

These blocks show the players' scores on the stage.

The ask and answer blocks

A sprite can put a question to the person at the computer by using the "ask" block. Anything typed as the reply is stored in the "answer" block, which can then be used inside other blocks just like a variable can.

```
when ⚑ clicked
ask (How much is the cactus juice?) and wait
next costume
think  join  answer  (?? That's daylight robbery!)
```

35 Add this code to the Penguin sprite to set the "RedInfo" and "BlueInfo" variables, which are displayed on the screen to show the scores.

Type a space before "Gems:" so that it doesn't form a single word with the player's name on the stage.

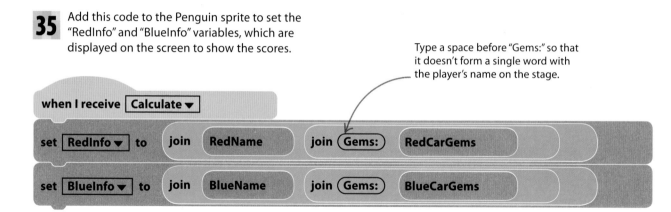

```
when I receive Calculate ▼

set RedInfo ▼ to  join  RedName   join (Gems:)  RedCarGems

set BlueInfo ▼ to  join  BlueName   join (Gems:)  BlueCarGems
```

36 Run the game. Hide all variables except "Countdown", "RedInfo", and "BlueInfo" by unchecking their boxes in the Variables section. Then right-click the RedInfo and BlueInfo signs on the stage and choose "large readout". To make everything look tidy, drag the signs to the top left and move the countdown to the top right.

Check the boxes to show the variables on the stage.

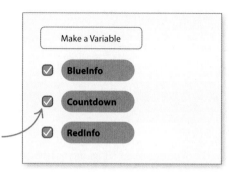

Make a Variable

☑ **BlueInfo**

☑ **Countdown**

☑ **RedInfo**

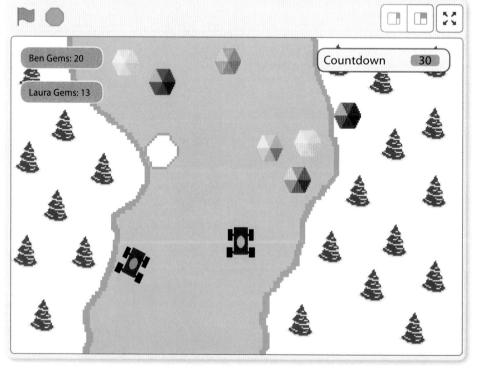

Ben Gems: 20

Laura Gems: 13

Countdown   30

• • • LINGO

String

Programmers call an item of data that contains words and letters a "string." It can include any character on the keyboard and can be of any length.

37 To make the penguin announce the winner, add the following code. This code has one "if then else" block inside another. Think about the three possible results—red wins, blue wins, and a tie—and it should all make perfect sense.

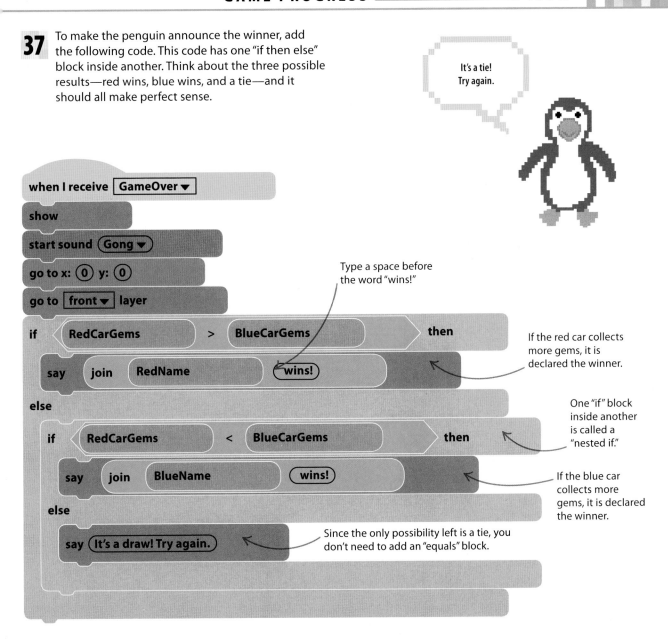

It's a tie!
Try again.

when I receive [GameOver ▼]

show

start sound (Gong ▼)

go to x: (0) y: (0)

go to [front ▼] layer

if ⟨ RedCarGems > BlueCarGems ⟩ then

   say (join (RedName) (wins!))

else

  if ⟨ RedCarGems < BlueCarGems ⟩ then

    say (join (BlueName) (wins!))

  else

    say (It's a draw! Try again.)

Type a space before the word "wins!"

If the red car collects more gems, it is declared the winner.

One "if" block inside another is called a "nested if."

If the blue car collects more gems, it is declared the winner.

Since the only possibility left is a tie, you don't need to add an "equals" block.

38 Finally, add some rhythmic dance music to make the game feel faster. Load "Dance Around" to the Game Loop sprite, and then add this code. It's a loop, and extra loops can slow everything down, but since it runs only once every few seconds, it won't affect the game play.

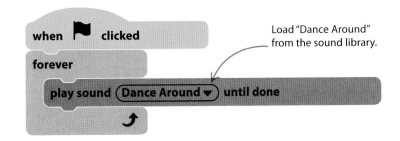

when ⚑ clicked

forever

  play sound (Dance Around ▼) until done

Load "Dance Around" from the sound library.

Hacks and tweaks

Now over to you! Personalize this race with your own features and adjustments. Make it as fast, slow, hard, serious, or silly as you like.

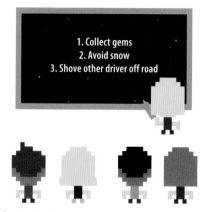

▽ **Record your own sounds**

You can use your own voice to make announcements in the game. To record your voice, you need a computer with a microphone. Select the Penguin sprite, and click on the Sounds tab. Then click the microphone icon in the sounds menu to make a recording. Replace the Penguin's "say" block with a "start sound" block and choose your recording.

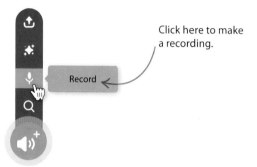

Click here to make a recording.

△ **Instructions**

Remember to add instructions to the project page in Scratch. Make it clear that it's a competition to get the most gems and not a race to the finish line. Give players a helpful hint by telling them they can push the other player off the road.

▷ **Fine-tuning**

To change how hard or easy the game is, adjust the "CarSpeed," "RoadSpeed," and "Countdown" variables that are set at the start. You can also adjust how long the cars spin after a crash, how big the bounce is when they collide, and how often snowballs and gems appear. Try to get just the right balance to make the game challenging but not too hard.

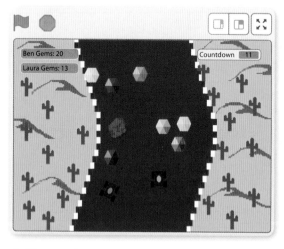

△ **Change the scenery**

It's easy to change the setting of Glacier Race by repainting the scenery. You can make the players race through a desert canyon or a dirt track in a forest. Remember to change the snowballs to match your theme.

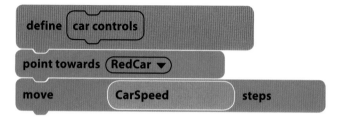

△ **One-player game**

Experiment with a one-player version of the game where you play against a computer-controlled blue car. First, save a copy of the project so you don't spoil the two-player version. Change the car controls for the blue car, as shown here, and then try the game. The blue car will chase the red car and crash into it.

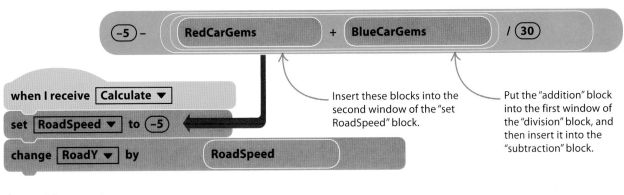

when I receive Calculate ▼

set RoadSpeed ▼ to -5

change RoadY ▼ by RoadSpeed

Insert these blocks into the second window of the "set RoadSpeed" block.

Put the "addition" block into the first window of the "division" block, and then insert it into the "subtraction" block.

△ **Need for speed**

For extra thrills, you can make the game speed up as players collect more gems. To do this, change the "set RoadSpeed" block in the Game Loop sprite so that the variable changes with each gem collected.

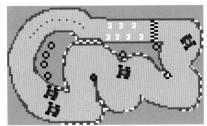

▪ ▪ ▪ **GAME DESIGN**

Camera angles

Game designers often talk about the "camera" in a computer game. This refers to how the picture on the screen follows the action in the game. There is no real camera, but if you imagine a camera capturing the action, you can think about different ways of showing what's going on. Here are some common camera views in computer games.

◁ **Fixed**

The camera watches all the action from one spot, without moving. Most of the games in this book use this simple camera, either with a side or bird's-eye view of the action.

△ **Tracking**

This camera follows the player around the game. In Glacier Race, the camera follows the cars, keeping them in view as the road moves by.

△ **First person**

This camera shows the view the player would see through their own eyes. First-person games make the player feel immersed in the action, instead of watching from afar.

△ **Third person**

This type of camera is positioned just behind the player's sprite. The player feels involved in the action but can clearly see what the sprite is doing.

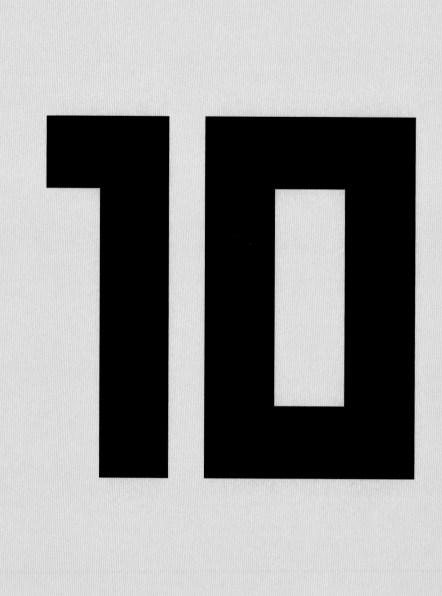

Tropical Tunes

How to build Tropical Tunes

Computer games aren't just about quick reflexes—they can also challenge your thinking powers. Here's a brain game to test how good your memory is.

Click the green flag to start a new game.

You score a point each time you click on the correct drum.

Score 30

AIM OF THE GAME

In Tropical Tunes, you have to listen to the drums play and then repeat the ever-growing tune. Make a mistake and the game's over. The longer you can match the tune, the higher your score.

◁ **Listen**
The drums play a tune, starting with a single note and then adding one new note each time.

◁ **Drums**
Click the drums in order to repeat the tune the game plays to you.

◁ **Game over**
Make a mistake and the game ends. As the tune gets longer, the game gets harder.

GAME CONTROLS

Use a computer mouse or touch pad to play this game.

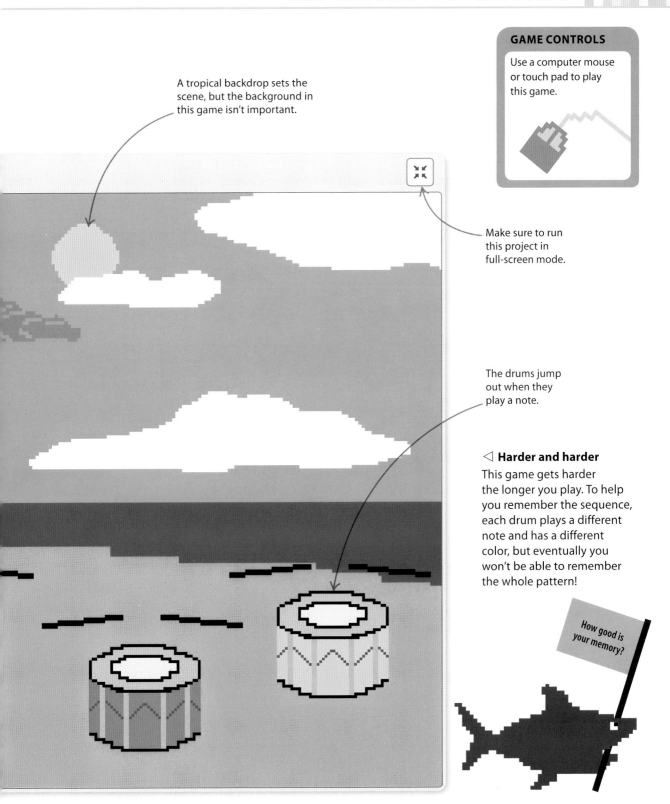

A tropical backdrop sets the scene, but the background in this game isn't important.

Make sure to run this project in full-screen mode.

The drums jump out when they play a note.

◁ **Harder and harder**
This game gets harder the longer you play. To help you remember the sequence, each drum plays a different note and has a different color, but eventually you won't be able to remember the whole pattern!

How good is your memory?

Make a drum

This game is quite complicated, so you'll need to work through the instructions carefully. To get started, follow the directions to make one drum with all the code blocks it needs. Once that's done you can copy it to make all four drums. Later, you'll create a game loop called the "master controller" to play the drums.

1 Create a new Scratch project and add or create any backdrop you want. A tropical theme works well with this game.

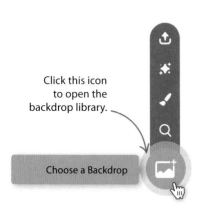

Click this icon to open the backdrop library.

Choose a Backdrop

2 The game needs four drums, but you can make just one to start with. Delete the cat sprite and add the "Drum" sprite from the sprites library. Drag it to the lower left of the stage.

The name "Drum" will be given to the sprite automatically.

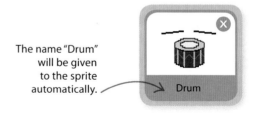

Drum

Two types of variables

You may have noticed the option to choose "For all sprites" or "For this sprite only" when you create a variable. So far you've mostly used "For all sprites", but you'll need to use both options in this game.

3 Before you can start making the code blocks that bring the drum to life, you need to create some variables. Click on the Variables section and make two variables for all sprites called "DrumToPlay" and "ClickedDrum". Uncheck their boxes. Every sprite in the game can use these variables.

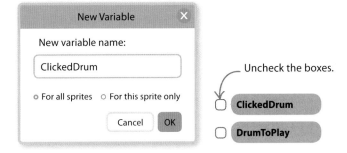

Uncheck the boxes.

☐ **ClickedDrum**

☐ **DrumToPlay**

4 Now add three variables "For this sprite only". Call them "drumColor", "drumNote", and "drumNumber". These variables will store information only about the Drum sprite: its number, its color, and which note it plays. Using "For this sprite only" enables you to copy this sprite to make more drums later, while allowing each drum to have different values for these variables.

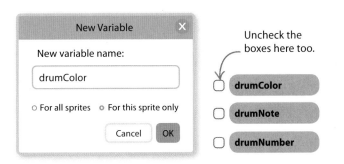

Uncheck the boxes here too.

☐ **drumColor**

☐ **drumNote**

☐ **drumNumber**

5 First add the Music extension, then build the code below for the Drum sprite. It sets up the drum's number, its color, the note it plays, and the type of sound it makes (like a steel drum). Run the project to set the variables and watch the drum change color.

This drum's variable information is set up in these three blocks.

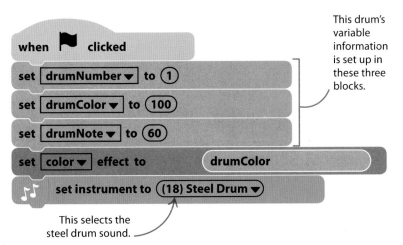

```
when 🏴 clicked
set drumNumber ▾ to (1)
set drumColor ▾ to (100)
set drumNote ▾ to (60)
set color ▾ effect to   drumColor
♪♪  set instrument to ((18) Steel Drum ▾)
```

This selects the steel drum sound.

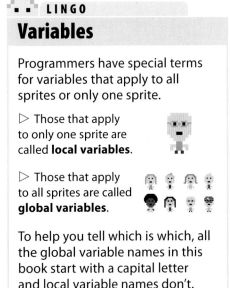

Making your own block

In Dog's Dinner and Glacier Race, you found out how to create your own customized Scratch blocks. You'll need to create a few more in this game.

Type the name of the new block in here.

6 Go to the blocks palette and select "My Blocks". Then click on "Make a Block" and a window will pop up. Type in the name of your new block, "play drum", and click "OK".

Click here.

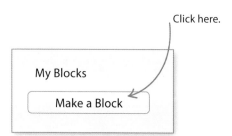

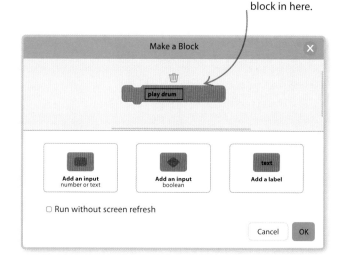

7 The new block appears in the blocks palette and a special pink header block, "define play drum", appears in the code area.

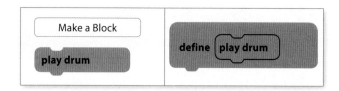

8 Build this code below the "define play drum" block. Then if you use the "play drum" block anywhere, Scratch will run this code. The code will make the drum grow in size, play a note, and then shrink back to normal. You can test the new "play drum" block by clicking on it.

9 Now add this short code to the Drum sprite. Click the drum on the stage to test it. Before testing, you'll need to click the green flag to set the value of drumNote.

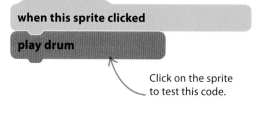

Click on the sprite to test this code.

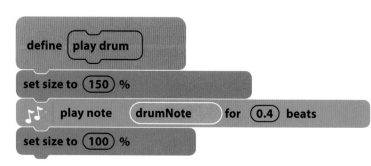

Remote control drums

Tropical Tunes makes the drums play a sequence that the player has to copy. The game controls the drums by using a master controller to send messages to them and then wait for a reply. Before you set up the master controller, give Drum the code blocks it needs to receive and broadcast messages.

10 Build this code, which will be triggered by a message called "RemoteControl". Create the message by clicking the drop-down menu on the "when I receive" block. Choose "New message" and type in "RemoteControl".

Create a new message called "RemoteControl".

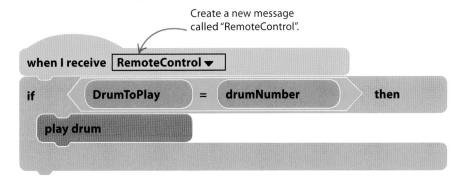

```
when I receive  RemoteControl ▼

if    DrumToPlay  =  drumNumber    then

    play drum
```

▽ **How it works**

Eventually there will be four drums numbered 1 to 4 (the local variable drumNumber). Before the master controller broadcasts "RemoteControl" it will set the *global* variable "DrumToPlay" to the number of the drum it wants to sound, and only the matching drum will play. We will add these steps later.

This variable for all sprites tells the game which drum to play.

```
set  DrumToPlay ▼  to  (2)
broadcast  (RemoteControl ▼)  and wait
```

Don't add these blocks yet—we'll use them later.

MESSAGE

Only Drum2 plays, because its "drumNumber" matches "DrumToPlay".

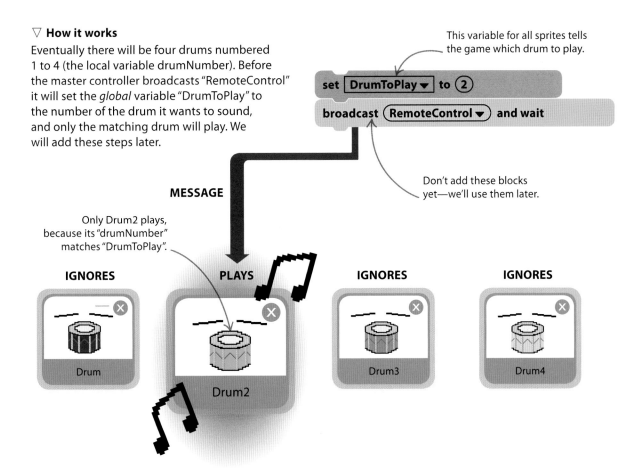

IGNORES — Drum

PLAYS — Drum2

IGNORES — Drum3

IGNORES — Drum4

11 When the player clicks a drum, the master controller will need to check it's the right one. To make this work, you need to make the clicked drum do two things. First, it will change the global variable "ClickedDrum" to its own number. Then it will broadcast a message to make the master controller run its check. Change the Drum sprite's "when this sprite clicked" code to look like this.

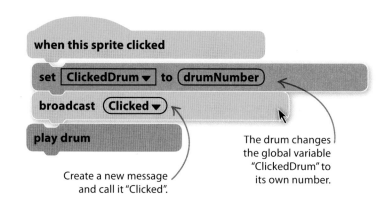

The drum changes the global variable "ClickedDrum" to its own number.

Create a new message and call it "Clicked".

Four drums

You now have one drum complete with its code blocks. You can copy it three times to create the four drums you need for this game.

12 Duplicate the drum three times, then change the values of the three local variables as shown below to give each drum a different number, color, and note. Arrange the drums on the stage, ordered from one to four.

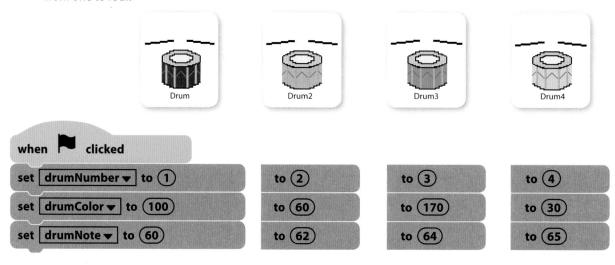

13 Now run the project. Each drum should become a different color. Click on them in turn to hear them play. If they move instead of playing, click on the full-screen symbol at the top right of the stage. Nothing else will work yet, but it's good to test that your drums all play correctly.

The master controller

Now you need to create the game's main brain: the master controller. The master controller broadcasts the "RemoteControl" message that plays the drums, but it does several other jobs too. It generates the drumbeat sequence the player has to follow; it checks that the player has clicked the right drum; and it keeps track of the score. It will need several code blocks to do all this.

14 The stage is a good place to put the master controller code blocks as they don't belong to any one sprite. Click on the stage info area at the bottom right of the Scratch window to choose the stage.

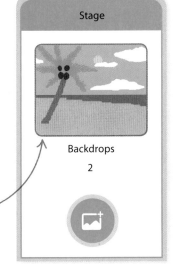

Click here to add some code to the stage.

15 The master controller will keep track of the ever-growing sequence of drumbeats by storing them in a numbered list. To create the list, open the Variables section and click the "Make a List" button. Name it "DrumOrder"—it's going to store the order in which the drums will play. Check the box so you can see it on the stage.

Check here to show the list on the stage.

16 With the stage selected, build this test code to generate a random sequence of seven drum numbers in the list. This code isn't part of the final game (for that, the code will need to add notes one by one). However, building it will show you how lists work and will let you try out the drums.

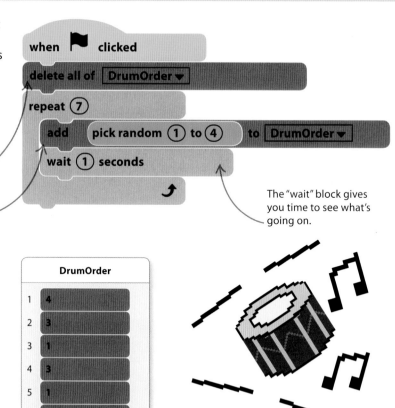

when 🏴 clicked

delete all of DrumOrder ▼

repeat 7

    add pick random 1 to 4 to DrumOrder ▼

    wait 1 seconds

This block clears the list at the start of the test.

This block adds a random drum number to the end of the list.

The "wait" block gives you time to see what's going on.

17 Run the code and watch the "DrumOrder" list on the stage slowly fill up. it will look like this, but your numbers won't be the same. The drums don't play yet because there are no blocks to tell them to.

DrumOrder

1	4
2	3
3	1
4	3
5	1
6	2
7	2

+   length 7   =

Lists

Making a list is a great way to store information, and lots of programming languages use them. They are handy for all sorts of things, from creating leaderboards and doing complex calculations to giving sprites artificial intelligence. In Tropical Tunes, we use a list to store numbers, but you can store words in lists too.

Lists are usually hidden, but you can display them on the stage just like variables.

You can use a list to make a sprite say something random when you click on it.

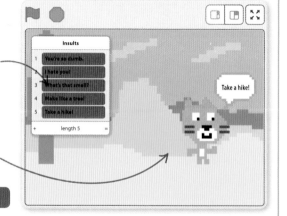

when this sprite clicked

say item pick random 1 to 5 of Insults ▼

Commanding the drums

18 Make sure the stage area is still selected. Now create another new block called "play sequence" and build the code shown here. It will play the notes in the list in order by traveling once though the blocks in the loop for each item in the "DrumOrder" list, setting "DrumToPlay" from the list, and then sending out the "RemoteControl" message.

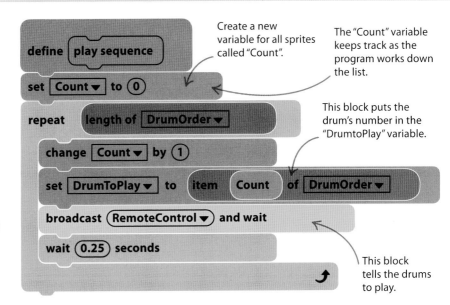

Create a new variable for all sprites called "Count".

The "Count" variable keeps track as the program works down the list.

This block puts the drum's number in the "DrumtoPlay" variable.

This block tells the drums to play.

19 Add the new "play sequence" block to the test code.

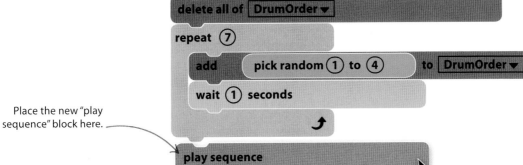

Place the new "play sequence" block here.

 **EXPERT TIPS**

Broadcast blocks

There are two types of broadcast Scratch blocks. They are useful in different ways.

broadcast (Message ▼)

broadcast (Message ▼) and wait

△ **Broadcast**
This sends the message but then continues straight to the next block without waiting. This is useful for triggering an event without stopping what's going on, such as launching an arrow without pausing the loop that moves the player's sprite.

△ **Broadcast and wait**
This sends the message but then waits until all receiving code blocks have finished before running the next block. This is useful when you don't want the code to continue until something's finished, such as the drum playing in this game.

20 Now run the code. Watch the numbers alongside the items in "DrumOrder" appear as they are read by the code, then hear and see the correct drum play each time. You can check the "DrumToPlay" variable's check box to show the number used with the "Remote Control" message for each note.

Select the check box to show the "DrumToPlay" variable on screen.

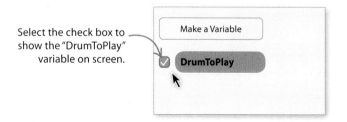

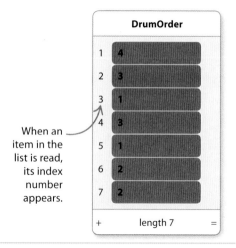

DrumOrder	
1	4
2	3
3	1
4	3
5	1
6	2
7	2
+	length 7 =

When an item in the list is read, its index number appears.

Adding notes to the tune

So far you've just been testing the drums. It's now time to get them playing the sequences needed in the game, starting with one note and adding another note each time the player repeats the tune correctly.

21 The test code isn't needed anymore so replace it with this one. You'll need to create another new block called "wait for player"—its code is shown in the next step. You'll also need to create a new variable for all sprites, called "Score", and check it so it appears on the stage.

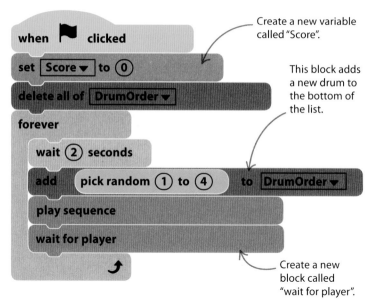

Create a new variable called "Score".

This block adds a new drum to the bottom of the list.

Create a new block called "wait for player".

22 Add a new variable called "CorrectCount" to count how many drums the player gets right. Then create this code, which holds up the loop while it waits for the player to get the whole drum sequence right.

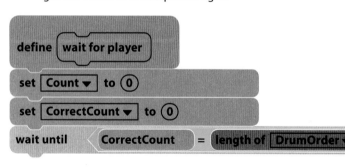

23 If you run the project now, the drums will play one note and then wait. You can click as many drums as you like but nothing will happen because you haven't programmed the master controller to respond to the "Clicked" message yet.

Checking the player's tune

Now you need to add some code to respond to the player's clicks on the drums. Every click creates a "Clicked" message that can trigger the code to check which drum was clicked and count the number of correct clicks. If the player clicks the wrong drum, the code will broadcast a "GameOver" message.

24 Add the next bit of code to the stage to increase "CorrectCount" by one for each correct click. When the drums are clicked, they play and send the "Clicked" message, having put their number in "ClickedDrum". This code will be triggered by that "Clicked" message. If the numbers don't match, the game ends.

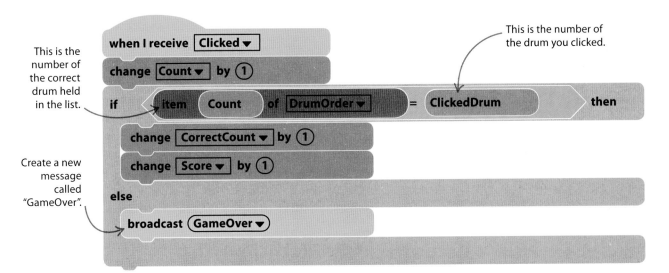

This is the number of the correct drum held in the list.

This is the number of the drum you clicked.

Create a new message called "GameOver".

```
when I receive  Clicked ▼
change  Count ▼  by  1
if    item  Count  of  DrumOrder ▼   =  ClickedDrum   then
    change  CorrectCount ▼  by  1
    change  Score ▼  by  1
else
    broadcast  GameOver ▼
```

25 Add some game-over code to the stage. You'll need to load the "Bell Toll" sound to the stage from the Scratch sound library.

26 The game is complete. Now try playing it, but remember to uncheck "DrumOrder" in the Variables section of the blocks palette or the player can just read the correct drum order off the list.

```
when I receive  GameOver ▼
play sound  Bell Toll ▼  until done
stop  all ▼
```

Uncheck the box to hide the drum order from the player.

Make a List

☐ DrumOrder

How it works

This game relies on two messages: "RemoteControl", which tells a drum to play, and "Clicked", which tells the master controller that a drum has been clicked by the player. The master controller has a loop that uses these two messages in turn—to play the tune and then check the player's reaction.

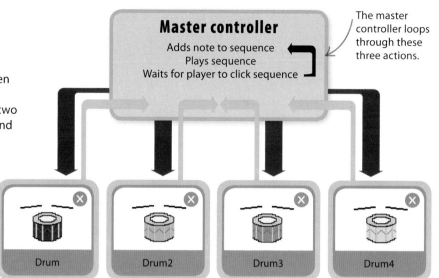

Master controller

Adds note to sequence
Plays sequence
Waits for player to click sequence

The master controller loops through these three actions.

 "RemoteControl" message makes the drums play.

"Clicked" message tells the master controller when a drum is clicked.

Drum   Drum2   Drum3   Drum4

Hacks and tweaks

Once everything is working smoothly, you can play around with the code and tweak the game to try and make it more exciting or harder. Here are some ideas.

Obey me!

△ **Talking shark**
Try adding a shark sprite that swims up and gives instructions—make him talk using the "say" block.

▽ **Another drum**
Add a fifth drum. You'll need to change its drum number, note, and color values, and check anywhere in the code that thinks there are only four drums—such as the random block in the master controller.

△ **Round counter**
Create a new global variable "Round" and show it on the stage. Set it to zero at the start of a game and increase it by one every time the player completes a sequence correctly (at the end of the master controller loop).

◁ **Game over**
Add a game-over sign or make the shark swim back on to the stage to say it.

Debugging

Bugs are errors in programs. Getting rid of them is called debugging. If a program isn't working properly, there are a number of common Scratch problems you can check for, which are shown below. If you're following instructions and something isn't working, it's also worth going back to the beginning and checking all the steps—there could be a small mistake in one of your code blocks that is affecting the whole game.

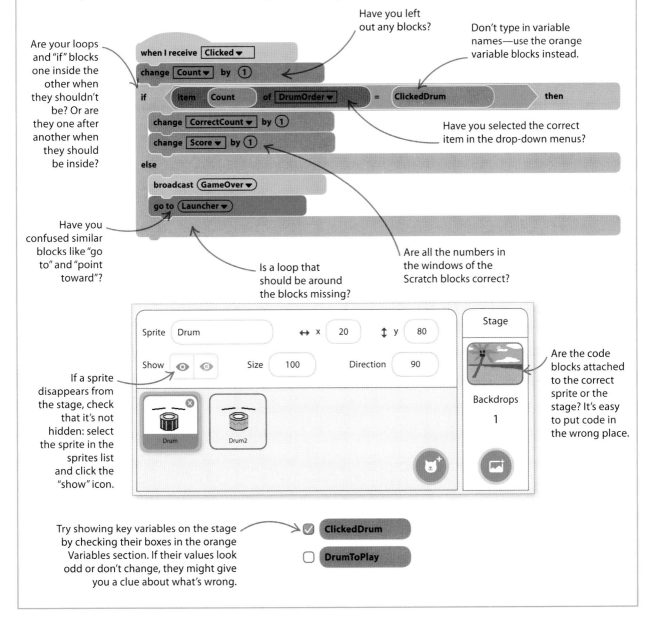

Have you left out any blocks?

Don't type in variable names—use the orange variable blocks instead.

Are your loops and "if" blocks one inside the other when they shouldn't be? Or are they one after another when they should be inside?

Have you selected the correct item in the drop-down menus?

Have you confused similar blocks like "go to" and "point toward"?

Is a loop that should be around the blocks missing?

Are all the numbers in the windows of the Scratch blocks correct?

If a sprite disappears from the stage, check that it's not hidden: select the sprite in the sprites list and click the "show" icon.

Are the code blocks attached to the correct sprite or the stage? It's easy to put code in the wrong place.

Try showing key variables on the stage by checking their boxes in the orange Variables section. If their values look odd or don't change, they might give you a clue about what's wrong.

What next?

Remixing and beyond

The Scratch website allows you to see other users' code and reuse it in your own games; this is called remixing. Millions of projects have been shared online and you can dive into every one. It's a great place to share your games and find ideas.

Exploring Scratch

To see games shared by other Scratch users, go to the Scratch website at **www.scratch.mit.edu** and click on Explore.

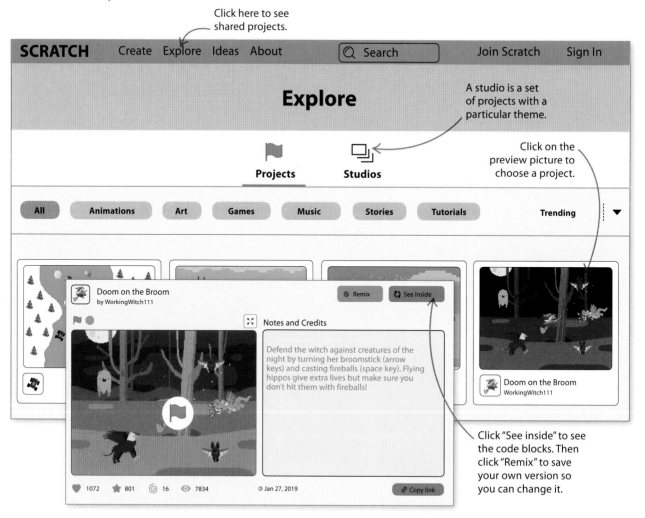

Click here to see shared projects.

A studio is a set of projects with a particular theme.

Click on the preview picture to choose a project.

Click "See inside" to see the code blocks. Then click "Remix" to save your own version so you can change it.

Creating your own games

Once you've built all the games in this book, you'll probably be bursting with your own game ideas. Here are some tips to help you get started.

1 **Big and small ideas**
Good ideas can come to you at surprising times, so be ready to jot them down before you forget them. Don't just keep notes about new games —write down ideas about smaller details such as characters, objects, levels, and actions.

2 **Beg, borrow, and steal**
People say the best ideas are stolen. Scratch allows you to steal ideas from everyone else, so go ahead. Look through other people's projects and save in your backpack any sprites, costumes, backdrops, sounds, or code blocks you like so you can reuse them later.

3 **Code your game**
Start with the basics. Begin by coding the main character so it works with your chosen controls (keyboard or mouse). Then build up slowly, adding one sprite at a time and creating the code it needs to play its part in the game.

4 **Testing**
Once you're happy with the game, ask someone else to play it. They might find problems that you missed because you know the game too well. Fix any bugs and make sure it all runs smoothly.

5 **Share it!**
Click the "See Project Page" button at the top of the Scratch editor and add a few words to explain how to play the game. Then click on "Share" to allow the whole world to play your masterpiece. Well done, you are now a game maker!

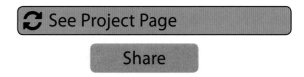

Better Scratch

Good programmers try to write code that's easy to understand and change. There are many ways in which you can improve your projects and expand your knowledge of Scratch. Here are a few of them.

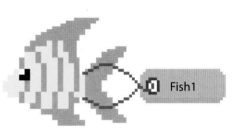

△ Use clear names

Scratch lets you choose names for sprites, variables, and messages. Make sure you use meaningful names, such as "Dragon" or "Score", to make your Scratch code readable.

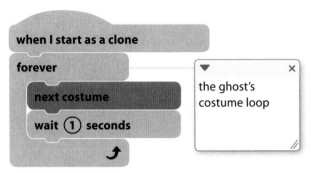

△ Comments

You can add comments to any block to explain your code. To do this, right-click (control click on a Mac) on it and select "Add Comment". This can remind you when you read code written a while ago.

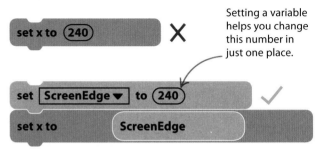

Setting a variable helps you change this number in just one place.

△ No unexplained numbers

Avoid writing code that contains unexplained numbers. To make your code easier to read, add a comment or use a variable so the number explains itself.

▽ Backpack

The backpack is a feature found at the bottom of the Scratch screen. It lets you store useful code blocks, sprites, sounds, and costumes and move them from project to project. But remember that you can only use it online.

Drag and drop a code block or sprite to copy it to the backpack.

Backpack

| sound Scream2 | costume monkey-a | costume Underwater 2 | script code |

Tutorials

Are you still unsure about how to use certain features? Scratch has many built-in tutorials for learning more of the basics.

1 Select the tutorials icon at the top of the Scratch window. A list of projects will appear. Look through them and choose what you'd like to work on.

Click here to go to the tutorial library.

2 Click on a tutorial to get started. Scratch will give you a step-by-step lesson that teaches the concepts.

Total number of screens in a tutorial.

Click here to end the lesson.

Click here to go back to the tutorial library.

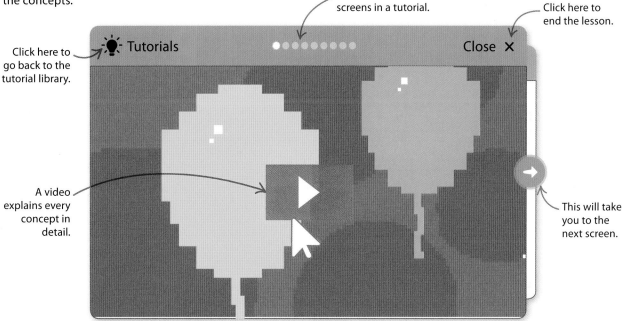

A video explains every concept in detail.

This will take you to the next screen.

Making your project different

Scratch projects often look and sound similar if you use only resources from the Scratch library. To make yours different, import your own images and sounds into Scratch.

Click here to use a sound file from your computer.

△ **Your own images**
You can import any image into Scratch, but don't share a project containing photos of people you know. You can also create your own images with a graphics program or the paint editor in Scratch.

Click here to use your webcam to take a picture.

△ **Your own sounds**
You can record your own music and sound effects through your computer's microphone and edit them in Scratch. You can also find free music and sounds on the web to use in your games.

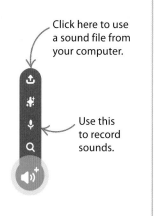

Use this to record sounds.

The next level

Once you've made a few Scratch games of your own, you may want to expand your horizons. There's a whole world of knowledge and experience you can tap into to improve your game design and programming.

Game design

Begin by improving your knowledge of games and how they're created. The following activities will expand your imagination and stimulate your game-design brain.

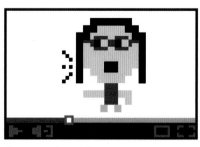

△ **Learn from the experts**
Many game designers love to talk and write about how they design games. You can find their tips on video-sharing websites and in blogs and magazines.

◁ **Play games**
Playing games can trigger ideas for new ones. Try out different games and watch other people playing them. Think about the actions (mechanics), rules, and goals that make a good game work. Imagine how you might code these different parts of the game yourself.

▷ **Find stories**
Ideas for games and the characters in them often come from stories. Next time you watch a good film or read a good book, think how you might turn it into a game.

▷ **Explore gaming history**
Find out more about the history of gaming. Visit a video game museum or a vintage arcade. There are lots of free online versions of famous video games, so it's easy to try classic games this way.

GAME OVER!

△ **Think visually**
Thinking visually is a vital skill for a game designer. Practice drawing or try making models. To help create animations, film someone walking and then pause the video during playback to see their posture changing.

◁ **Keep notes**
Keep a notebook of game ideas, drawings, stories, and anything that you find fun or interesting—you never know what might be useful later. You could even start a blog about gaming to share your ideas with friends and family.

Programming

To make computer games, you need to know how to code. Brushing up on your coding skills will help you make better games.

▷ Sharpen your Scratch

Try the tutorials and explanations on the Scratch website. Learn everything you can about Scratch and you'll be able to code things you never dreamed possible.

△ Code together

Join or start a coding club at your school or library. Collaborating on projects with other coders is a great way to fire your imagination and supercharge your skills.

▷ Learn another language

Scratch is a great springboard to learn other programming languages, such as Python or JavaScript. There are lots of online coding courses, including some that focus on games. Python has a great add-on called Pygame that helps you create games.

△ Try a game engine

You don't have to build computer games from scratch—you can use programs called game engines to do a lot of the difficult coding for you. You can find game engines online. Many can be tried for free.

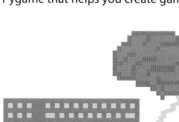

◁ Do your research

If you have a technical mind and want to learn more about the latest advances in computer games, read up on 3-D graphics, game physics, and artificial intelligence.

EXPERT TIPS

Game engines

A game engine is a program that contains already-made code for building games. It works a bit like Scratch, but it's designed for professional game developers instead of beginners learning to code. Game engines provide easy ways to detect controller inputs and to guide sprites around the screen. Solutions to problems caused by collision detection and game physics are built in. Game engines can also convert games to run on consoles and mobiles, saving you the nuisance of rewriting all the code.

Jobs making games

Some computer games are created by a single programmer, but others are put together by huge teams. The computer games industry employs thousands of people. Most of them specialize in just one part of the process.

Who makes games?

Game studios are companies that make games and employ specialists to work as a team. On smaller games, each person usually has more than one job. On a big project, there might be dozens of programmers and artists, each working on just a small part of the game.

△ **Producer**
The person in charge of a project and all the people working on it is called a producer. It's the job of this producer to make sure the game is the best it can be.

△ **Writer**
The stories and characters in a game are developed by writers. In a game with cutscenes (short, movielike sequences), the writer is responsible for what the characters say.

△ **Game designer**
The game designer creates the rules, goals, and mechanics that make a game interesting and fun for players. Playability is the designer's main focus.

◁ **Artist**
Everything the player sees—the characters, objects, and scenery—are created by artists, often working as a team under a single lead artist.

LINGO

Game types

Indie games Short for "independent games", these are created by people working on their own or in small teams. Many feature creative new ideas not seen in mainstream games.

AAA games These are the biggest games and are expected to sell millions of copies. They take many months or even years to make and have huge teams and budgets of many millions of dollars.

△ **Composer**
A composer is a professional musician who writes new music. Good music is vital because it helps create atmosphere in a game.

△ **Sound designer**
The sound effects in a game help to set the scene. They are created by a sound designer, who also decides how the composer's music will be used in the game.

△ **Programmer**
Programmers take all the ideas and building blocks created by the team and use them to write code that makes the game work.

△ **Tester**
It might sound like a dream job playing games all day, but it's a serious and important part of developing a game. A tester has to play the game over and over to check if it works correctly and is not too easy or hard.

△ **Game publisher**
Some games have a publisher, a company that pays for the game's development and then advertises and distributes the final product.

Game development

Games go through lots of different versions before the final one is released for sale. The early versions take the game from a basic idea to a finished product and usually follow the sequence shown here.

 GAME DESIGN

From blocks to riches

In 2009, Swedish programmer Markus "Notch" Persson released the first version of Minecraft, a building game he'd made. By 2014, Minecraft had around 100 million registered users and was sold to Microsoft for $2.5 billion.

1 Prototype
The prototype is an experimental version of the game built to see if the basic idea works and is fun to play.

2 Alpha
The alpha version has all the main features, but they might not be fully working. They are improved and major bugs are fixed before the next stage.

3 Beta
The beta version of the game has everything, but it needs polishing and still has minor bugs, which need to be found and fixed.

4 Release
The release is the final version, fully tested and fixed. Some games are available as "early access" releases for fans to test before the game is 100 percent finished.

Have fun!

Games can transport you to different worlds and take you through a whirlwind of emotions, but the most important part of gaming and making games is to have fun.

Party time!

Playing games with people is much more fun than playing on your own. Why not grab some snacks and invite your friends around to play your favorite multiplayer game? You could also get them to try out games you've made in Scratch and ask them to suggest improvements. They might even want to create their own versions.

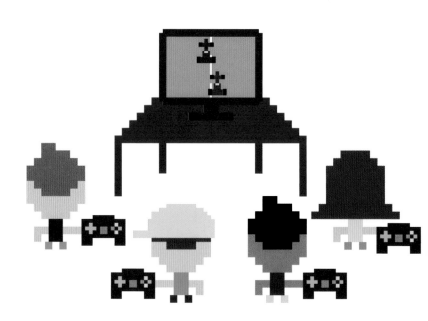

Hold a game jam

A game jam is a game-making party. People get together for a day or two to race against time as they build a game from start to finish. Every year, countless game jams take place. Some take place in a single location, but others are scattered across the world and linked through the internet or even held entirely online. Why not hold a mini Scratch jam at your home or school? Pick a theme and ask a teacher or parent to help arrange computer access, judging, and prizes.

▷ **Choose a theme**
Game jams usually have a theme, such as "jumping games" or "games with bees in them." Prizes are awarded for building the best games.

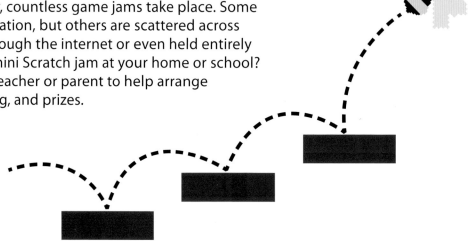

Challenge yourself

It's good to push yourself sometimes, so why not set yourself a game challenge? It could be anything from making a fully playable game in just 15 minutes to making a game for every letter of the alphabet. You could also keep a diary or blog to describe your experiences, or create a Scratch studio to share your challenge games.

Find or start a game club

If your school or library has a coding club, you can ask them to run some sessions on game design and programming. Start a group within the club for people who have a special interest in making games.

 EXPERT TIPS

Game idea generator

For some people, the hardest part of creating games is having the idea for a game in the first place. Here's a trick to help give you inspiration. Roll a die to choose a number from each column, and then combine the results to generate a random game idea. Feel free to change it—it's just to get your creative brain in gear!

Genre	Setting	Extra feature
1. Maze	1. Forest	1. Patrolling enemies
2. Jumping	2. Space	2. High score
3. Quiz	3. Underwater	3. Collecting objects
4. Vehicle simulator	4. City	4. Life counter
5. Virtual pet	5. Castle	5. Time limit
6. Interactive story	6. Beach	6. Multiplayer

Glossary
and Index

Glossary

algorithm
A set of step-by-step instructions that perform a task. Computer programs are based on algorithms.

animation
Changing pictures quickly to create the illusion of movement.

artificial intelligence (AI)
Programming to make characters such as enemies in a game appear to behave in intelligent ways.

assets
All the pictures and sounds used in a game.

backdrop
The picture behind the sprites on the stage in Scratch.

backpack
A storage area in Scratch that allows you to copy things between projects.

block
An instruction in Scratch that can be joined to other blocks to build code.

Boolean expression
A statement that is either true or false, leading to two possible outcomes. Boolean blocks in Scratch are hexagonal instead of round.

branch
A point in a program where two different options are available, such as the "if then else" block in Scratch.

bug
A coding error that makes a program behave in an unexpected way. Bugs are named after the insects that got into the wiring of early computers, causing errors.

camera
The imaginary camera through which a player views a game.

code
A stack of instruction blocks under a header block that are run in order.

collision detection
Programming that detects when two objects in a game are touching.

condition
A "true or false" statement used to make a decision in a program. See also *Boolean expression*.

console
A computer that is used just for playing games.

costume
The picture a sprite shows on the stage. Rapidly changing a sprite's costumes can create an animation.

data
Information, such as text, symbols, or numbers.

debug
To look for and correct errors in a program.

directory
A place to store files to keep them organized.

event
Something a computer program can react to, such as a key being pressed or the mouse being clicked.

execute
See *run*.

export
To send something to the computer from Scratch, such as a sprite or a whole project saved as a computer file.

file
A collection of data stored with a name.

flag
A variable that is used to pass information from one sprite or code block to another.

function
Code that carries out a specific task, working like a program within a program. Also called a procedure, subprogram, or subroutine.

game engine
A program that helps a programmer make games by providing already-made code for many common game features, such as animation, controls, and game physics.

game jam
A competition in which game makers race against the clock to build the best game.

game loop
A loop that controls everything that happens in a computer game.

game physics
Programming to create forces and collisions between objects in a game.

genre
A type of computer game. Platform games and first-person shooters are common genres.

global variable
A variable that can be changed and used by any sprite in a project.

graphics
Visual elements on a screen that are not text, such as pictures, icons, and symbols.

GUI
The GUI, or graphical user interface, is the name for the buttons and windows that make up the part of the program you can see and interact with.

hardware
The physical parts of a computer that you can see or touch, such as wires, the keyboard, and the screen.

header block
A Scratch block that starts a bit of code, such as the "when green flag clicked" block. Also known as a hat block.

import
To bring something in from outside Scratch, such as a picture or sound clip from the computer's files.

index number
A number given to an item in a list.

input
Data that is entered into a computer. Keyboards, mice, and microphones can be used to input data.

integer
A whole number. An integer does not contain a decimal point, nor is it written as a fraction.

interface
The means by which the user interacts with software or hardware. See *GUI*.

library
A collection of sprites, costumes, or sounds that can be used in Scratch programs.

list
A collection of items stored in a numbered order.

local variable
A variable that can be changed by only one sprite. Each copy or clone of a sprite has its own separate version of the variable.

loop
A part of a program that repeats itself, removing the need to type out the same piece of code multiple times.

mechanics
The actions a player can do in a game, such as jump, collect objects, or become invisible.

memory
A computer chip inside a computer that stores data.

message
A way to send information between sprites.

network
A group of interconnected computers that exchange data. The internet is a giant network.

operating system (OS)
The program that controls everything on a computer, such as Windows, macOS, or Linux.

operator
A Scratch block that uses data to work something out, such as checking whether two values are equal or adding two numbers together.

output
Data that is produced by a computer program and viewed by the user.

pixel art
A drawing made of giant pixels or blocks, mimicking the appearance of graphics in early computer games.

pixels
The colored dots on a screen that make up graphics.

procedure
Code that carries out a specific task, working like a program within a program. Also called a function, subprogram, or subroutine.

program
A set of instructions that a computer follows in order to complete a task.

programming language
A language that is used to give instructions to a computer.

project
Scratch's name for a program and all the assets that go with it.

random
A function in a computer program that allows unpredictable outcomes. Useful when creating games.

recursion
See *recursion*.

run
The command to make a program start.

Scratcher
Someone who uses Scratch.

server
A computer that stores files accessible via a network.

software
Programs that run on a computer and control how it works.

sprite
A picture on the stage in Scratch that code blocks can move and change.

stage
The screenlike area of the Scratch interface in which projects runs.

statement
The smallest complete instruction a programming language can be broken down into.

string
A series of characters. Strings can contain numbers, letters, or symbols such as a colon.

subprogram or subroutine
Code that carries out a specific task, working like a program within a program. Also called a function or procedure.

variable
A place to store data that can change in a program, such as the player's score. A variable has a name and a value.

Index

Acknowledgments

Dorling Kindersley would like to thank: Bahja Norwood for editorial assistance and testing; Caroline Hunt and Steph Lewis for proofreading; and Helen Peters for the index.

Dorling Kindersley India would like to thank Riji Raju for editorial assistance; Abhijit Dutta, Aadithyan Mohan, Priyanka Sharma, and Mark Silas for code testing.

Scratch is developed by the Lifelong Kindergarten Group at MIT Media Lab. See **http://scratch.mit.edu**